becoming all things

HOW SMALL CHANGES LEAD TO LASTING CONNECTIONS ACROSS CULTURES

michelle ami reyes

ZONDERVAN
REFLECTIVE

ZONDERVAN REFLECTIVE

Becoming All Things
Copyright © 2021 by Michelle Ami Reyes

Requests for information should be addressed to:
Zondervan, 3900 Sparks Dr. SE, Grand Rapids, Michigan 49546

Zondervan titles may be purchased in bulk for educational, business, fundraising, or sales promotional use. For information, please email SpecialMarkets@Zondervan.com.

ISBN 978-0-310-10891-7 (hardcover)
ISBN 978-0-310-12456-6 (international trade paper edition)
ISBN 978-0-310-10893-1 (audio)
ISBN 978-0-310-10892-4 (ebook)

Published in association with Don Gates of the literary agency The Gates Group, www.the-gates-group.com.

Cover Design and Art: Juicebox Designs
Cover Image: Shutterstock
Interior Design: Denise Froehlich

To Aaron, my co-trailblazer.
Can you believe this moment is here? You and I began our
exploration of cultural identities together. I wouldn't want
to cross worlds and create new spaces with anyone else.

To those with bicultural and multicultural identities
who have found their way to this book.
The spaces we've created were always meant
for you. This is your moment. Rise up
and lead us into a glorious future.

Though I am free and belong to no one, I have made myself a slave to everyone, to win as many as possible. To the Jews I became like a Jew, to win the Jews. To those under the law I became like one under the law (though I myself am not under the law), so as to win those under the law. To those not having the law I became like one not having the law (though I am not free from God's law but am under Christ's law), so as to win those not having the law. To the weak I became weak, to win the weak. I have become all things to all people so that by all possible means I might save some. I do all this for the sake of the gospel, that I may share in its blessings.

—1 Corinthians 9:19–23

Contents

Foreword

Several years ago, my wife and I joined a group traveling to Israel to tour the land of the Bible. We may never forget some of the sights and sites. The Bible became three-dimensional as we stood on the Temple Mount, the Mount of Olives, and the ruins of a synagogue in Capernaum. We found ourselves inside a world we had only read about and imagined—imagined, as it turns out, without sufficient inspiration!

But as much as we enjoyed the ruins, landscape, and food, the trip would not have been as life-changing without our tour guide, Yuval. Yuval was a second-generation tour guide, having learned at the foot of his father, who led tours for decades. Born Jewish, he was born again through faith in Christ at some point in his early adulthood. As a lifelong resident of Jerusalem, he also knew Arabic and was familiar with historical and contemporary Israeli-Palestinian conflicts. He brought all of that knowledge to our tour.

But he also brought something else—interest in us and

some familiarity with our cultures. Yuval became a bridge between worlds as he became all things to all of us. Yuval transformed our time from a potential series of "stones and bones" tourist traps into a deep-water immersion filled with complex cultural, religious, political, and historical perspectives. We walked the land with glimpses through his eyes. We toured the land, but we also toured his thought, feeling, and experience, and in that tour, we saw ourselves afresh.

An excellent tour guide does that for you—she or he *narrates* life in a way that draws you in and even redefines you.

We need excellent tour guides to help us navigate our way through the landmarks—and landmines—of our cultural identities and experiences. We need help with the narration of life, someone to help us realize we have stories and we tell them selectively. We need someone to help us examine that selectivity to discover what we're leaving out and how it shapes our identities and perceptions. We need someone to help us notice the details we would otherwise miss. Someone to tell us the stories that make the "monuments" meaningful. Someone to open our minds, hearts, and eyes to others on the journey so we benefit from their perspective and contribute to their lives in meaningful ways.

Crucially, most white Americans, for most of American history, have never taken a tour of their own cultural and racial identities. They have never had a guide point out details or give meaning to them. Just as crucial, most people of color, for most of American history, have had to negotiate multiple and sometimes competing narratives. They've had to define themselves in relationship to one community and to assert counterdefinitions in relationship to another community. The hopeful assessment of this reality might be something like this: God has been preparing people of color to help white people understand that white is a color and white people have a culture. This is a crucial mission because when white people fail to understand this, they often do alarming damage to people of color. American history is filled with examples.

We desperately need to be led by a skilled interpreter, a guide who knows the terrain and the stories hidden there, someone sensitive to the human heart—to their own heart and the heart of others.

The Lord has graciously gifted my sister Dr. Michelle Reyes with a heritage, upbringing, education, and gifts to serve the church as a much-needed guide. She will tell you her story of being a "tweener"—someone not quite at home in the multiple cultures she navigates. From that perch, she helps us escape the Black-white binary to see more of the kaleidoscope of identities we share and experience. She will bring to bear the Bible, theology, sociology, and history. Those who listen to her guidance will begin to see themselves differently and to interact with the world more effectively.

As I read this book, I became aware of how few guides we really have in the church. Further, I became aware of how rarely we listen to the handful of guides we do have. This two-fold problem makes this book both rare and urgent. It makes reading and applying this book both necessary and an act of repentance.

Michelle writes with a prophetic clarity we need to heed. Those who heed this calling will find hope and help from someone who has been experiencing and thinking about who we are, our stories, and the possibility of a deeply informed, justice-loving, gospel-motivated, apostle-imitating, multiethnic unity all of her life. It's time we end the centuries-long, country-wide commitment to "whiteness" as the standard for culture, identity, and meaning and begin a lifelong pursuit of discovering what it means to have the *imago Dei* as the standard for culture, identity, and meaning. It is past time to take off the old man and put on the new. It is time to embrace becoming all things to all people. This book helps you do that.

Thabiti Anyabwile
Washington, DC

Introduction

Commit to Change

As an Indian American woman, I've learned to live my life like a chameleon. I'm constantly changing my identity based on who I'm interacting with because, more often than not, I am the sole Indian in a non-Indian space. I grew up in an all-white town and attended an all-white school. I've never been a part of an Indian community, and I've never been a part of the majority. Never. I'm a woman of color with a bicultural identity, and I can't escape my reality. My only recourse has been to learn to blend in seamlessly wherever I go.

Being able to mold myself to the people around me is a unique skill. Even now, I instinctively withdraw when I enter a new space and ask myself, "Who am I? Who do others want me to be?" These questions play on repeat in my head as I silently observe which words and gestures are welcome and which are not. I pay close attention to social cues and cultural expressions so that I can adjust how loud I am, how many of my emotions I can share, and which personality traits I can express. I play a role, and often quite well—with success being measured by how positively the person I'm with treats me in return. But this process can also leave me tired and discouraged. I wonder what the real me would look like, and whether I could be different, whether I could stick out of the crowd and still be accepted.

Then again, being able to transform is also one of my greatest strengths. I know how to make someone feel seen and understood. My radar for people on the margins is keen, and I'm passionate about making sure people don't get left behind. I understand the pain of feeling unwelcome in monocultural spaces because I've been there. I've walked that path before, and I can extend a hand of friendship to say, "I got you. Let's do this together."

Being able to adapt culturally, to change who I am for the people around me, is not the life I would have chosen for myself, not at first anyway. Growing up, I spent most of my days just trying to fit in. I wanted to be loved and have friends. It's perhaps the most a brown-skinned Christian girl like me could hope for, growing up in a Scandinavian community in Minnesota. I lived in a world of in-betweens, where I wasn't considered Asian, but not white either. I was like no one and was constantly aware of the ways I stuck out. So I spent much of my childhood thinking something was wrong with me and actively trying to make my Indianness invisible. I desperately tried to imitate my white classmates so that I would be more likeable or prettier, or at the very least so that someone would start sitting by me at the lunch table. I thought that being Christian meant being white and that I needed to alter my cultural identity to be accepted.

I told myself I just needed to make the best of it. If I could figure out how to act like the cool kids, dress like the pretty girls, do my hair the way they did, or talk the way they did, then maybe they wouldn't make fun of me in class anymore, exclude me from parties, or say my culture was weird. Fitting in would somehow be worth no longer wearing Indian clothes outside the home, bringing homemade lunches to school, or distancing myself from familial narratives and values.

But that all changed after college. In the time it took me to leave Minnesota and pursue a doctoral degree in downtown Chicago, Christians of color started becoming more visible, raising their voices, and stepping into leadership roles, both within the church and outside of it. That, along with the immediacy of social media, helped me connect with people more like me. I discovered a world of people with bicultural and multicultural identities, who had all grown up like I had, living in the in-between, constantly renegotiating their identities, and trying to make it one day at a time. I was no longer alone. It didn't matter if we were Black, Brown, or white; we were learning to see the beauty in our cultures and to embrace the plurality of our expressions. We could be like everyone and yet still celebrate our uniqueness.

These were the early days of my cultural identity development. In these last few years, the topic of culture and cross-cultural engagement has risen to the forefront of everyone's consciousness. Cultural identities and cross-cultural relationships can no longer be ignored, least of all by Christians. Those who have been journeying on this road have stories of pain and joy to share. Others are stepping into this for the very first time.

The more we speak up about, acknowledge, and process what we are learning and experiencing, the more we see that we're all at different places in our journeys. Some people are realizing for the very first time that whiteness and white American culture are real, and they are wrestling with the reality and confusion of racial differences between themselves and people of color. Some people of color carry hurt, anger, and trauma for the ways they've had to accommodate to the dominant culture and hide aspects of their cultural identities. Being asked *yet again* to step into a place of vulnerability and openness feels like an impossible task. Still others have tried to extend a hand of friendship across cultures and have experienced criticism or shame in the attempt. Where do we go from here?

Connecting across cultures might feel a bit daunting, but you are reading this book because you want to keep trying. You know something isn't working and you're willing to try something new. Healthy relationships across cultures are possible. Majority and minority, Black, Brown, and white, can come together and thrive. I've seen it and experienced it. But the road forward begins with a willingness to embrace change. We must be willing to think differently about who we are and the way we're supposed to live. We must learn how to be culturally adaptable and read Scripture through this lens. That is the goal.

Consider the life and identity of the apostle Paul. Paul was both a Jew and a Roman citizen. He had a cultural duality that made him unique, and this enabled him to connect with people of different ethnicities, languages, and socioeconomic statuses. Paul could talk with Jews in the synagogues and discuss philosophy with Greeks in the public square. He regularly crossed borders to meet new people, and though his underlying convictions did not waver, he adopted different approaches toward circumcision and dietary laws depending on who he was with. For Paul, to be a follower of Jesus meant that he lived a life of constant cultural adaptation, and his willingness to embrace change made him particularly well suited to form cross-cultural relationships. Paul embraced his cultural identity, yet he knew how to step outside of it because he saw his ability to be adaptable as a strength. His motivation to connect across cultures wasn't driven by a need for survival, but rather a deep understanding of who God had made him to be and a love for all peoples.

Paul writes about cultural adaptability throughout his epistles, but the verses that best summarize his thinking are found in 1 Corinthians 9:19–23:

> Though I am free and belong to no one, I have made myself a slave to everyone, to win as many as possible. To the Jews I became like a Jew, to win the Jews. To those under the law I became like one under the law (though I myself am not under the law), so as to win those under the law. To those not having the law I became like one not having the law (though I am not free from God's law but am under

Christ's law), so as to win those not having the law. To the weak I became weak, to win the weak. *I have become all things to all people* so that by all possible means I might save some. I do all this for the sake of the gospel, that I may share in its blessings. (emphasis added)

Let's focus on the phrase "I have become all things to all people." Every time I read these words, I think about my own life. The very thing I felt forced to do growing up—becoming different things with different groups of people—is here presented positively, as a fundamental aspect of the Christian life. The challenge to become cultural chameleons isn't just for Indian Americans like me. It's true for all Christians everywhere. We all need to hear Paul's words and think about what they mean for us today. Imagine him saying right now, "To the African American, I became like an African American. To the Mexican American, I became like a Mexican American. To the Native American, the Asian American, the Afro-Latino, the Anglo American, the Chicano, the Cuban, the Nigerian, the Cherokee, the first-generation Guatemalan immigrant and the sixth-generation Chinese American, I became like each and every person for the sake of the gospel." Each of us is called to go on a journey of becoming all things to all people. Becoming is not code for appropriating or stealing other people's cultures. It is a posture that desires to see the world through other people's eyes, values what they value, and both centers and honors their way of life. This will require humility and flexibility. We all need to learn what it means to adapt and transform ourselves to better love and serve the people around us. This adaption isn't optional. It's not just for the overseas missionary. It's the call for every Christian.

The more you believe this truth, the more you will see it play out in Scripture. Moses, the Hebrew, grows up in the Egyptian court, and God raises him up as a spokesperson for his people with unique access to Pharaoh. Ruth, a Moabite, marries into a different culture and comes to play a crucial role in the story of Israel as the great-grandmother of King David. Esther, a Jewish woman in Babylon, knows how to address a king and utilizes the art of storytelling to save her people. In the book of Numbers we read about the biracial priest Phinehas. Professor of Old Testament J. Daniel Hays explains that the name Phinehas "translates as 'the Negro,' the 'Nubian,' or 'the Cushite': that is, one of the Black people who inhabit the land of Cush."[1] Phinehas is a dark-skinned African. He also happens to be the great-nephew of Moses (Aaron's son Eleazar marries a daughter of the Egyptian Putiel; Exod. 6:25). What makes Phinehas unique is that he embodies the message of God not by hiding his cultural identity but by embracing it to speak a message to God's people that an ethnic Jew wouldn't have been able to convey. He is an outsider speaking to God's people, and that makes him good at his job.

Many of the men and women in the Bible learn to change and adapt their words, personalities, and lifestyles to connect with the people around them. And Jesus is no exception to this pattern. In fact, the incarnation is a perfect model of cultural embodiment. Jesus came to this earth as a brown-skinned, first-century Jewish man. The eternal Son of God transformed himself, despite pain and hardship, to meet us on our terms. He embraced another nature to become like those he loved and navigated different languages (Aramaic and Greek) as well as different sociopolitical contexts (Jewish and Roman). He adapted to human culture, acquired our customs, languages, and pains in order to care for, heal, save, and unite us. Salvation was his goal, but the first step in saving us was crossing into our world and meeting us where we lived.

When talking about Jesus's cultural identity, it's important to understand that Jesus was not white. He didn't have fair skin or look like a white American man. Not only is Jesus Jewish, but he has a complex, multicultural heritage according to the Gospel of Matthew. New Testament scholar Andrew Rillera writes, "Only Matthew mentions women in Jesus's lineage, and he significantly includes great-grandmothers who were foreigners (Tamar, Rahab, Ruth, and Bathsheba; Matt 1:5–6). Some come from nations that are Israel's paradigmatic archenemies: the Canaanites (Tamar, Rahab) and Moabites (Ruth)."[2] This diverse heritage informs not only Jesus's identity but also how he engages with the world. Jesus's multicultural roots allow him to seamlessly cross cultural divides and show love equally to Jews, Romans, Samaritans, Canaanites, and others in ways that are fundamentally non-Western and non-Eurocentric.

Christ is our example. But following him will not be simple. If cultural adaptability came with a high degree of pain for Jesus, you can be assured your journey will not be easy either. Some of us will struggle more than others. In fact, adapting to other cultures might be easier for me as a bicultural woman than someone who has never stepped outside of their monocultural space before. And that's okay. In the book of Acts, Paul easily and fluidly adapts to different people groups in a way that the apostle Peter does not. Peter has far more bumps along the road. He picks fights, and Paul has to help put out a few of his fires. But God uses those bumps to stretch and grow us; that's part of the learning process too.

Learning to adapt to different cultures in our heads, hearts, and bodies won't be easy, but it will get *easier* over time. Each of us has to commit to a process of change and commit to persevering because the work is hard and the road is long. We have to believe, truly believe, that living out the gospel means continually changing ourselves within different cultural contexts to better love and serve the people around us. At the heart of the Christian life is a commitment to a messy web of cross-cultural relationships that seeks the flourishing of all people, whether that be within our own families, our neighborhoods, our churches, or our society as a whole.

So be encouraged. You can do this. We can do this. And we can do it together.

Chapter 1

Develop Your Cultural Identity

"Why do you talk about culture so much? I mean, shouldn't you be talking more about our unity in Christ than our cultural differences?"

I was in mid-bite of a delicious salami and Gouda sandwich, picnicking with some old college friends. Our kids were playing nearby in the grass, and we had just finished talking about diapers and sleep cycles when one of my friends dropped this question on me. I immediately had a sinking feeling in my stomach. It's not that I didn't have an answer to the question. I just didn't know if I wanted to answer.

Conversations about faith and culture require a good deal of mental and emotional energy. I have to gauge how much the person posing questions knows about the topic and how much information I should supply. I've been navigating this issue for a long time. I've dedicated my career to writing and speaking on the topic. Yet many people, including the husband and wife asking me the question at that moment, haven't thought much about it. I know they love Jesus and mean well, but I'm also aware they know almost nothing about the topic. The churches they attend don't talk about faith, ethnicity, and culture. They don't listen to, follow, or read anything by Christians of color. My husband and I are the only friends of color they have. But even more than that, I'm trying to discern whether their question comes from a desire to listen and learn or if they just want to debate or put down my ideas.

I'm not picking on them simply because they're white. But I've been having more and more of these same conversations with white Christians since 2017 when one of the most visible and influential minority evangelicals in the United States, the artist Lecrae, left conservative evangelicalism over cultural differences.[1] Some Christians today still don't understand why a person of color would no longer want to identify as evangelical. Some white Christians feel like African American, Native American, Asian American, and Latino/a (among many other) believers are making too much of their cultural identities. Yet these same white Christians also can't understand why, after years of dialogue, the chasm between minority Christians like myself and my white brothers and sisters is still growing.

Many white Christians don't realize that Lecrae's divorce from white evangelicalism was a watershed moment for many minorities. Many of us had spent years feeling like the outsider, like something was wrong with us, and that we should remain silent if we disagreed with our white friends on an issue. I knew I didn't fit the image or the lifestyle of many white Christians, but there was no space for that in our conversations. However, when Lecrae made his personal frustrations public about the historic disconnect between evangelical faith and culture, I thought, "Oh, we get to talk about this now?" For many of us, the floodgates suddenly burst wide open.

Since then, I've grown bolder in talking about my identity and my past, about the ways my faith and culture intertwine, and how my experiences are different from those of white evangelicals. But so often, I am misunderstood. When I bring up topics like cultural differences or ethnic identity, I'm told that I'm being divisive, emphasizing things that shouldn't be an issue for Christians, and going against the grain of Christian unity, albeit a unity that aligns with the status quo of white evangelicalism.

So when my friends questioned why I was always talking about our differences instead of our unity, I knew this was a layered question. They were suggesting that my faith—and even my way of life as a Christian—should be acultural. In their minds, different cultural expressions of faith breed disunity and division among Christians. They were hinting that it was time to set aside my "dangerous elevation" of the culture card and instead embrace a "noncultural" expression of the faith, one that could unify all Christians.

"Isn't that what Galatians 3:28 says?" they asked. "'There is neither Jew nor Gentile, neither slave nor free, nor is there male and female, for you are all one in Christ Jesus.' If that's true, then our only distinctive as believers should be Christ."

Many of my fellow friends of color no longer engage in these discussions because for too long we've had to defend the legitimacy of our experiences. In addition, we've been unduly burdened with the task of teaching white people terms and histories, answering their questions, and speaking on behalf of all people of color everywhere. It's physically, emotionally, and spiritually exhausting. I wish it didn't have to be this way. At the very least, I wish my white friends had more friends of color so that other people could lovingly challenge them and open up space for these conversations. But I haven't given up yet. I'm still hoping and praying that God will use conversations like this one to change people's hearts and open eyes to new perspectives. So I dove in.

"You know what I hear when you say that? I hear you telling me that I need to hide my Indianness if I want to call myself a Christian."

A look of confusion washed over their faces. "No, you can be Indian," they replied, "We're not saying that."

So I elaborated: "Sure, it's okay if I wear a trendy Indian shirt or if we check out a vegan Indian restaurant for dinner. But what if I told you that my Indianness makes me see the world differently than you? I value things that you don't. I feel uncomfortable in places that are normal to you. Even our definitions of friendship are different."

Memories and experiences immediately flooded my thoughts. And I wanted to share it all. I wanted to somehow roll out my life like a movie reel so I could point out every difference, every pain, every moment of isolation. But I also knew that would be like a tidal wave, and I didn't want to overwhelm them. So I began trying to explain what it's like to be a minority in a majority culture.

"Do you know that almost every white friend I've ever had assumes we live our lives the same way? But we don't.

The truth is I've learned to hide certain aspects of myself, certain parts of my Indianness, around people with white skin because I'm tired of being misunderstood. My life revolves around talking and acting one way in a white context and another way in a brown context. Honestly, I'd like for you to know more of me, but I'm weary from continually having to explain and defend myself."

My friends grew defensive. They interjected and told me that I had it all backward. "Michelle, do you honestly believe there's more than one way to be a Christian? Everyone who follows Jesus is required to live their lives a certain way, no matter our cultural background."

At this point, we were talking past each other. I told them that when I hear "there's only one way to be Christian," I hear them saying that everyone should be like *white* Christians. But this idea didn't go over so well. It was met with a quick defense. Of course they weren't saying that. But now they're annoyed because to them it feels like I'm demonizing white people. They make sure I know they attend a diverse church, which for them is a clear sign they value more than just white culture.

But as most people of color know, there's a big difference between a true embrace of diversity and tokenism. I affirmed what I could, while also pointing out the problem: "You say diversity is important, but when does diversity go beyond valuing faces with different skin colors? When do people actually embrace different opinions, behaviors, and expressions? Things like how I read the Bible, my views on justice, the poor, and immigration, and what I think is okay and not okay to say about other people. I think what you really want is for people of different ethnicities to think like you do and to prioritize the same things as you. I can be Indian as long as my life doesn't challenge yours in any way."

I wanted to say more. I could've said more. But my friends were not convinced. We had come to an impasse, and they asked if we could just agree to disagree. I nodded my head, mostly because I was tired and discouraged. What level of intimacy can our friendship have if we don't agree on something so basic—that our cultural differences inherently shape how we follow Jesus?

Redefining Terms

Part of the reason for the confusion we experience in these conversations on culture stems from our yearning for unity. Countless times I've heard people try to downplay cultural differences by saying things like, "We don't have a culture," in an effort to make their churches, homes, or communities feel *more* welcoming. But this approach inevitably fails, and worse, it isn't informed by a biblical understanding of culture. Yes, Christians all believe in "one body and one Spirit, just as you were called to one hope when you were called; one Lord, one faith, one baptism; one God and Father of all, who is over all and through all and in all" (Eph. 4:4–6). These are the truths of Scripture. But these truths aren't read, believed, and practiced in a vacuum. They are *always* culturally expressed. The message of salvation is for every people group. What God has done in Jesus crosses ethnic groups and generational differences and is for everyone for all time, but it is *always* contextualized from one culture to the next.

This is difficult for many people to accept, largely because we fear the dangers of subjectivity. We don't want the message of salvation or our theology or what it means to belong to Christ to be just *a* truth and not *the* truth. We are nervous about going down a path that implies any particular belief is right or any action is good because it's part of a particular culture. So we reduce the cultural aspect of a belief or a message to the outward clothing that covers the unchanging essence of the gospel. It's the wrapping that delivers the message.

But what exactly is culture? Is it really just an external addition, like the clothing we wear?

The term *culture* is one of the most difficult words in the English language. We all have different definitions for this term, and scholars and thought leaders debate its meaning. So I want to be clear about what I mean when I use it. When I refer to *culture*, I'm referring to the narratives born from our individual ethnicities.[2] This is, to some extent, a new way of understanding culture. The term *culture* traditionally has been used to group whole communities and nations together. However, as new research suggests, that simple conceptualization is no longer applicable within our hybridized global landscape. Dr. Georgia T. Chao and Dr. Henry Moon effectively argue that culture should be used as a construct to distinguish individuals.[3] Each of us carry different layers of culture within ourselves. In other words, each of us have a unique cultural narrative, which, as professor of anthropology Brian Howell explains, is a composite of the complex stories we pick and choose from our communities, including our families and our friends, that helps us determine what it means to live a good life and to be a good person. These stories tell us what is normal and right, what is human and what is not. At my core, I've collected, organized, and created a unique story that guides the choices I make and the interests I have. My story is similar to those of other Indian Americans, but it is also uniquely my own. The same is true for you. If you were to write down what you think is good, beautiful, and important in this world, you'd be formulating your own cultural narrative that is both similar to and distinct from that of your cultural community.

Culture as a narrative system is the definition I recommend you begin to use in your day-to-day life. It's particularly helpful if you want to have healthy cross-cultural relationships. Seeing culture as a narrative leads us to appreciate each person for who they are instead of valuing them based on where they're from or what they do. Our approach to culture should never be merely about nationality, ethnicity, geographical location, language, or material items like food and clothing. All of these markers are fluid and can change. They are also less applicable when people of a certain cultural group live across the world and have blended multiple cultural elements into their lives. Culture is also not about the systems humans can build. Though the English word *culture* stems from the Latin word *cultura*, meaning to cultivate, develop, or grow, the assumption that humans are defined by what they create immediately turns the conversation toward biological theories of evolution and who is able to progress the most—an approach that, throughout history, has threatened human dignity and has flattened diversity and creativity among people groups, especially subdominant cultures.

Cultural narratives, on the other hand, are stories formed and maintained by individuals about ourselves and the world around us. They are stories imbued with ideals and principles regarding family, honor, assertiveness, hard work, and communal living, and they become the glue that holds our way of life together. My cultural identity also inevitably leads to certain cultural expressions. To put it simply, the story of who I am informs the way I live my life. And we begin to understand the spiritual significance of our stories when we look at how culture develops and functions in Scripture.

Seeing Culture in Scripture

When we turn to Genesis and the first accounts of recorded Scripture, we see that you cannot separate culture from creation. In the creation account we read, "So God created mankind [*adam*] in his own image, in the image of God he created them; male and female he created them" (Gen. 1:27). Here the first humans are simply called *adam*, or humankind. God doesn't create a specific race of people. There is no mention of Adam and Eve being Hebrews or Egyptians or Canaanites.[4] We can't even infer a particular skin color, such as whether they are white, Black, or Brown. This is a racially generic human who represents all of humanity—all peoples of all ethnicities and cultures—and we can infer from this that God created all peoples to reflect the image of God. We are all cultural image bearers. Every culture—with its unique bodies, voices, thoughts, actions, and values—in some way reflects God himself. As difficult as our cultural distinctives can be in relating to one another, we must always remember that one of the greatest ways in which we see the rich and vibrant beauty of our God on display is in the people he created. Moreover, each of our cultural expressions should be equally cherished. There is no particular culture that is superior or inferior. No matter your ethnicity, skin color, or cultural values, you have been made as a bearer of God's image with dignity and worth equal to every other person. If you don't value your cultural identity, you are not valuing a vital aspect of the image of God within you. If you don't value the cultural identity of another person, you are not valuing the image of God within him or her.

This picture of human beings as cultural image bearers is further illustrated in the genealogies of Genesis 5 and 10. Both of these texts describe the lineage of human beings in ethnic-linguistic terms. In Genesis 10 the "Table of Nations" maps out the descendants of Noah from the line of Seth, and here we see how God's image bearers spread into the world and develop distinct cultural identities. Going throughout the world and developing unique ethnic narratives is, yet again, a fundamental aspect of what it means to be human.[5]

The story of the Tower of Babel in Genesis 11 is connected to the cultural commentary of Genesis 10. Too often God's dispersal of peoples at Babel is read as a curse. Some have even argued that the diversity of people groups and languages is the direct result of human sin. However, if we properly understand the cultural mandate of Genesis 1:28 and 9:1 to increase and fill the earth, we see that God's plan from the beginning of human history is to promote the spread of different people groups with different languages and ethnicities. The problem in Genesis 11 is that human beings have stopped spreading and diversifying, preferring to congregate in one place and unify around something other than God. Professor of Old Testament and Hebrew Dr. Bruce Waltke explains that, when read together, Genesis 10 and 11 hold a tension of two opposing aspects: "the unity of the tribes and nations as of one blood under God's blessing and their diversity into many languages under God's wrath"[6] The dispersing of peoples at Babel in Genesis 11 is simply God's intervention to continue his plan in creation—his push to further spread, multiply, and develop diverse ethnic identities.

In Genesis 1–11 we uncover a theological statement about God's vision for humanity, his intent to create us with cultural embodiment, and his desire for us to thrive and flourish together. This does not mean that every cultural identity is free of sin. Because we live in a broken, corrupt world, we must recognize that brokenness extends to our cultures too. Our cultural stories and narratives—and the values, beliefs, and meaning we associate with them—are also imbued with human sin. That's what makes all of this very complicated. If our cultural identities are a product of our humanity, rooted in both the *imago Dei* and the fall, then part of learning to embrace our cultural identities and value them means also learning to differentiate what is good and right from what is an idol. We can be proud of who God made us to be without weaponizing that pride to think less of other people and how they live. We can value our unique cultural stories and expressions without worshiping the products of our culture. In all our cultural stories we must address the problem of sin while never losing sight of the vision of cultural harmony in Genesis 1–3. Adam and Eve had cultural identities that were created to be good, holy, and in right relationship with God, and the same is true for you.

With that in mind, let's return to the argument that some Christians make based on Galatians 3:28 that our cultural identities don't matter if we are "in Christ." They point to the phrase "There is neither Jew nor Gentile" as the basis for this view. However, this logic isn't applied to the other concepts in this verse. For example, it also says that in Christ there is neither male nor female. Should this be taken to mean that everyone in Christ should now be asexual? Of course not. Our sexuality is fundamental to our creation in the image of God, and it courses through every part of our biblical worldview from Christology to marriage. Claiming that we should embrace a sexual neutrality would deny our distinctive diversity as men and women, including our biological differences, among other things. So if Paul isn't intending to negate sex in Galatians 3:28, we should not assume that he is seeking to negate diverse cultural identities either.

In fact, in this passage and throughout his epistles, the apostle Paul continually emphasizes cultural identities as part of the Christian faith and encourages Christians to respect cultural differences. God created us to have cultural identities—they are how we were made to see and engage the world in unique ways. And contrary to a surface-level reading of this verse, Paul is stressing in Galatians 3:28 and throughout his letters that we need to lean into these identities while learning how to enjoy and connect with those who are different from us.

This is why it's important to read a verse like Galatians 3:28 in dialogue with Paul's other texts on faith and culture, such as 1 Corinthians 9:19–23. This latter passage more fully explains what Paul believes, serving as a linchpin to his entire discourse on the subject. It's one of the reasons we will be studying the passage throughout the rest of this book. Here Paul writes, "To the Jews I became like a Jew, to win the Jews. To those under the law I became like one under the law (though I myself am not under the law), so as to win those under the law. . . . I have become all things to all people so that by all possible means I might save some" (vv. 20, 22). Once again, Jews and Gentiles are brought up (the Gentiles are those "not having the law"). But what does he mean? Paul is advocating for followers of Jesus to embrace cultural flexibility with the people they meet instead of trying to flatten cultural diversity. Rather than negating cultural identity, Paul is asking that we be willing to adapt how we express our cultural uniqueness as we interact with the world around us. You can't read 1 Corinthians 9 and still think Christians are supposed to be acultural. The missiological impulse in this passage argues the opposite—that you can't strip culture from people. If you could, you wouldn't need to do the hard work of becoming like them.

When we hold Galatians 3:28 and 1 Corinthians 9:19–23

side by side, we see that our cultural identities still matter when we become followers of Jesus. We remain a Jew or a Gentile, just as we remain a man or a woman. These passages also imply that we must go to great lengths to *become a servant to every other culture.* Though Paul is a Jew, no single cultural identity or narrative defines him. Rather, he fluidly adopts different customs to serve the people he works with. Being "in Christ" doesn't mean that we detach ourselves from our cultural identity. It also doesn't require a commitment to being colorblind. Instead, it means embracing cultural narratives that are different from ours. The emphasis in 1 Corinthians 9 is not on flattening our narratives into one single generic story, but on hybridity, on living as an embodied cultural being while also seeking to adapt culturally to different places with different peoples. Our gospel presentation hinges upon our ability to become all things to all people. Cultural intelligence is the measure of how well we, as Christians, are able to effectively present the gospel to others.

These ideas are brought home in the book of Revelation. There we see that cultural flourishing is paramount to our ability to be together in Christ not only in the present age as the church but also throughout eternity. The writer of Revelation, John, presents a picture of believers as multiethnic and multicultural, coming from all the nations of the earth to worship God together. This picture envisions the full conversion of the nations to obedience to Jesus, all while returning to Genesis 1 and the original intentions God had for creation. In Revelation 7:9, we see "a great multitude that no one could count, from every nation, tribe, people and language, standing before the throne and before the Lamb. They were wearing white robes and were holding palm branches in their hands." Around the throne of God one will find Ugandans, Mongolians, Arapaho, Vietnamese, Russians, Argentinians, Polynesians, South Africans, Koreans, Iranians, Bulgarians, Hmong, Mexicans, and a host of other peoples from thousands of different tribes and nations.[7] This is a picture of the ideal humanity with each person retaining their ethnicity, story, and voice as they unite in worshiping God for eternity. This vision of the future should impact how we see things today.

Revelation gives us a clear indication that the cultural identities we have now will continue in the new heavens and the new earth. And it affirms that from the very beginning of creation God intended a multicultural body of Christ. God created us, as people, to be diverse. This was his plan from the very start.[8]

Developing Cultural Identities

The rest of this book focuses on how to appreciate and adapt to other peoples and cultures. But we can't get there unless we first learn to see and embrace our cultural identities. Each of us needs to understand *what* our culture is and *how* it shapes our life, including what we believe and how we live out our faith. We will struggle to connect with someone else's cultural story if we don't understand our own.

Start Seeing Culture

This is the first hurdle for all of us. I'll put it bluntly—too often *whiteness is seen as an absence of culture.* I've had several white friends who don't think they have a cultural identity. Just recently, an Anglo American friend called me up on the phone to talk about this. She shared that she doesn't think about her cultural identity as she goes about her day. I remember her saying, "I don't think about my culture every time I talk to my neighbors or go to the store. I can't really imagine you do either."

That's the conclusion I hear almost every single time I talk about this with a white friend.

To be clear, I don't have anything against my white friends. I really don't. But let me tell you why I see statements like this as a problem. *Not having to think about your own culture is an ignorance born of privilege.* If you're part of the dominant culture, you don't have to constantly think about your culture because you are figuratively swimming in it. It's all around you, and it just feels normal. More than that, many white Americans assume their reality is the same for everyone else. This sense that the culture of white Anglo Americans is the norm, the accepted reality for everyone, is part of the problem. It's one reason most white people do not know their own cultural narrative, and it also leads to colorblindness. Colorblindness, as author Sarah Shin explains, "assumes that we are similar enough and that we all only have good intentions, so we can avoid our differences." However, given the viral explosion of racial unrest and ethnic tension in our country over these past few years, we're seeing that "our stories are different, and those differences cannot be avoided."[9]

Many minorities living (and often isolated) within the dominant culture also try to transcend cultural differences.

I've heard minorities say things like, "I'm a Christian who happens to be Black," or "I'm a Christian first and a Latina second." Often what fuels these ideas is a belief in and pursuit of conformity. In our country, some minorities want to prove that they are no different from their white brothers and sisters. They want to conform to the culture of white evangelicalism, either because they've been in majority spaces for so long that they're no longer aware of their own cultural heritage or because they live under the ideological weight that white is right and fear not fitting in. Whatever the reason might be, this mindset fails to elevate and affirm the goodness and holy intent of people of color being exactly who God made them to be and expressing their faith accordingly.

Living in a colorblind world is not the goal. Our cultural identities make up the unique and wonderful parts of who we are. To not see color is to not truly see or understand a person. Malcolm X once said that "Black is beautiful."[10] I agree! There is beauty in every skin color, story, and cultural value. Each of us must grow in our awareness of and appreciation for our own cultural identity and the cultural identities of others. Think about it, learn to see it, and then embrace it. This is who God has made you in his image, and being that person is how we become fully alive as children of God.

Think about What You Need to Learn or Unlearn

With this first point in mind—that every unique cultural identity is good and valuable—I want to clarify a second point for those who are white. Whiteness isn't a culture. It's a racial construct and a belief that people with white skin have greater value than people who are Black and Brown. "Being white" should never be seen as something to attain or a goal to be valued. Instead, learning to value your cultural identity means delving into your family's specific history. You are more than just an abstract, generic individual in the American melting pot. We all came from somewhere. Learn about your ethnic heritage and the specific people in your ancestry. Consider your roots. How has your family migrated around the world? What languages do they speak? What are some of the attitudes, mindsets, and values embedded within your ethnic heritage? What are the stories your family and community have passed on to you? What cultural knowledge do you value?

Part of your cultural identity development will involve a journey of first and second knowledge. By "first knowledge" I mean where you are right now, the things you've passively accepted to be true. These could be statements that downplay your cultural identity like "I don't have a culture," or "I don't see color." These are the ideas you need to unlearn and replace with a theologically richer "second knowledge" about the uniqueness of your family's (and community's) story and the narrative that informs your specific cultural identity. People with lighter skin tones, or as my friend Dorena Williamson writes in her book *ColorFull*, "vanilla-colored skin," have God-given cultural identities just like everyone else,[11] and there is an equal capacity for beauty in these cultural identities too. Lean into your ethnicity and your story. Learn to believe that it's only by embodying who God has made you—including your cultural identity—that you will fully and authentically be you.

For people of color reading this, I know that some of you might feel more white than Brown. Many of us have been taught that it's better, or at least easier, to embrace a white American cultural narrative. Maybe your skin tone is lighter, or your family's names were anglicized at some point in your past. You may even enjoy feeling like you can blend in with the majority culture. But what is *your* story? Who has God made *you* to be? As people of color, we need to start by admitting and acknowledging that we are not white. If we are one of the few minorities in a predominantly white space, we need to figure out how to have a healthy relationship with our own cultural identity.

This starts by learning how to unassimilate and become more comfortable talking about, centering on, and advocating on behalf of our culture. We need to go on a journey of tracing our ethnic roots and both learning and valuing the stories our community, our family, and our friends express. Who are the heroes of our community? What do people who share our ethnic and cultural heritage celebrate? What values can we take pride in? There is strength and uniqueness in your cultural identity, and God is inviting you to retell your story through this lens.

I would be remiss not to acknowledge the pain in this process. Many of us are displaced. Our identities are disconnected from a specific place, and we may not be able to trace our family's physical heritage beyond the last generation or two. Some families have shed their stories and values as they sought to assimilate and fit into white American society. You may have to go digging, and the more you uncover in your cultural narrative, the more wounds and scars you may uncover as well. The traumas and losses of one generation are often passed on to the next, and the pains of our ancestors, even our own parents, can become our pains too.[12] Healing and resilience will be necessary milestones on this journey.[13] It will take time. The process will be slow. Be gentle and patient with yourself.

No matter who you are or where you are in this journey, recognize that your narrative will also capture inchoate and sometimes contradictory elements. Because we live in a globalized society and have gleaned knowledge from a wide variety of places, many of us will think and embody things that don't really fit together. There will be some chaos in your story that can shape how you act and react, speak, and think. You might even think to yourself at some point, "Who I am doesn't make any sense." You're not alone. In all of our narratives there is both beauty and uncertainty, order and chaos, and that's part of the journey too.

Accept That Your Cultural Identity Shapes Your Faith

Finally, we need to consider how our cultural narratives shape our faith. I can tell you right now—you and I probably don't share the same views on what it means to be a follower of Jesus. We likely differ on how to do church and what it means to fellowship as the body of Christ. When you and I pray, we likely emphasize different characteristics of God and interpret the experience of suffering differently. We probably have different opinions on evangelism, missions, justice, what it means to be a good neighbor, and how to read and interpret the Bible. The variance in our points of view is not just the product of different theological training and personalities. It is evidence of different cultural narratives at work and how our cultural identity shapes our faith.

So let me ask you this: What does it mean for you to be a Christian? What have you been taught about the way you're supposed to think and live your life as a follower of Jesus? What do you consider appropriate and inappropriate? And what would you say are the most important aspects of your faith? Sit down and write out the answers. As you do, consider how your faith is informed by and expressed through your own cultural identity.

We will each express our faith differently *because of* our cultural narratives. These differences are not bad. As director of the Global Diaspora Institute at Wheaton College Sam George argues, we must embrace a concept of "Christianities"[14] so that we can acknowledge the real and good diversity of the Christian faith. The image of believers fellowshipping together in Christ throughout all eternity is a mosaic of cultural diversity, values, and stories. There's nothing uniform about it. It's time for each of us to see the many colors within the body of Christ and to celebrate the distinct role that each of us plays in crafting this masterpiece.

Chapter 2

Move beyond Stereotypes

I was sitting between a fridge of kombucha and a stranger's French bulldog and wishing I had stayed home. I was at a party where it was clear I wasn't fitting in. It wasn't just that there were no more seats available in the living room and I was stuck alone in the kitchen. I had been struggling all evening to find something—anything—to talk about with the people there. No one seemed interested in talking about the topics I gravitated toward, and in a room full of predominantly Anglo Americans I was starting to feel like a foreigner.

I felt far from home, the sole brown-skinned woman in a sea of white. Pretending like I was enjoying myself, I sipped on my fermented drink and laughed as jokes were made. But it didn't change the sense of isolation I felt. Sitting alone in a group is uncomfortable for anyone, and especially for people of color who have spent most of their life being placed in a corner.

As I was looking for an excuse to leave, to my surprise one

of the guys in the living room walked over to talk. Perhaps sensing my discomfort, he seemed to have come over to make me feel more at ease.

"You're Indian, right?"

I smiled nervously, took a deep breath, and nodded yes. But immediately I was wishing I could be alone again. I never know what is going to follow that question, and I was already bracing myself for whatever came next.

"Man, that's so cool," he replied. "I love India."

Yup. I've heard that one before. I never know exactly how to respond. Should I say, "I love India too"?

I'm sure this man had good intentions and didn't mean to associate my personhood with an entire country. But it's a conversation starter that always falls flat. The truth is that I was born in South Carolina and have lived most of my life in the United States. The one exception to this was a three-month doctoral residency in Berlin, Germany. India isn't even the mother country for my own mother. While she is ethnically 100 percent Indian, she was born and raised in an Indian village in Uganda, Africa. Some of my Indian friends are first-generation immigrants in the United States who have come straight from India. But I also have friends who were born in places like Guyana, Panama, and Trinidad and Tobago, and they have never been to India. Not once. What many people fail to realize is that ethnicity and nationality no longer correlate. Many of us who are ethnically Indian do not see India as "our country," and when people try to connect with me by talking about a nation that has never played an important role in my life, things get awkward.

In my experience, when someone says I love [fill in the blank with a whole country], they usually know very little about the people who live there or that culture—a fact that was quickly confirmed in this conversation as well.

He continued, "You know, it's funny, because I wasn't sure if I should ask you about India or not. You don't really look that Indian."

Now I really wanted to leave. But I was literally stuck between a kombucha and a hard place, and I had nowhere to go. Truth be told, he wasn't the first person to say this to me. I've grown up in a world where people constantly mistake my identity. The plight of many Indian Americans is that we are confused with other ethnicities—Iranians, Iraqis, Mexicans, and Turks to name a few. Even worse, this mistaken ethnic identity is often followed by various degrees of shaming and rejection. I've been accused of being a terrorist. I'm regularly given pat downs at airport security. I've been denied service at restaurants. I've been called "Pocahontas" and far worse. I do my best to shrug off these experiences, to pretend they don't hurt, but they do. Deep down I long to be known, understood, and valued for who I am.

Back to the party. I knew what this guy meant. I didn't look like the Indians he'd seen on the cover of *National Geographic* with dark skin, round faces, and long black hair. "Yeah," I said, "that's because my mom's family is originally from the state of Gujarat in western India. Indians from that area have lighter skin than Indians who live in the south." As the words came out of my mouth, I could see the rising disinterest in his eyes. I sensed he had come over to talk more out of curiosity than a genuine interest in getting to know me. I considered mentioning that I was also learning to like fermented drinks, but I figured it was probably pointless by now.

This is a common, repeated experience for many ethnic minorities: when someone attempts to make a connection, they stereotype and filter my cultural identity through what they know. We've all done this, and usually we do it without an intent to harm or insult the person. But there has to be a better way to navigate cultural differences. There has to be a better point of connection between a white man who *thinks* he knows something about Indians and a bicultural Indian American woman who doesn't check off any of his preprogrammed categories.

I am a unique individual. Rather than assuming I can be known or understood by assumptions made on the basis of my skin color or appearance, I want people to understand how my cultural identity informs the way I see the world. Yes, I want others to see my Indianness, and I want that to be visible, but not hypervisible. The color of my skin should not be the sole defining feature of my interaction with others. I want people to learn more about *my* favorite Indian foods. I want them to ask how I feel about hospitality, open doors, and communal gatherings. I want them to ask what it means to have grown up in a high honor culture, where we respect our elders and see the world through a communal lens. And sometimes I'd prefer to just talk about soccer or politics or the latest show I watched on Netflix because all of these things—and more—are part of what it means to be uniquely me, not whether I was born in India or if I look like the typical Indian (whatever that means).

In most situations, I try not to take offense when I engage in conversations like this one unless I know the person is openly mocking me (which happens on occasion). I get it. It's natural for us to try to find points of connection, and we need to show grace to one another during inevitable misunderstandings. Still, the way we go about making these connections is critical, and we can do better. A relationship will not thrive when the conversation stays mired in surface-level stereotypes about a culture or ethnicity. You can't just tell an Indian that you like curry and think you've bonded. Cross-cultural relationships with other people go beyond cultural stereotypes and involve getting to know an individual and their unique story and experience. Don't assume you know how they feel about their culture or ethnic background. Get to know them as a person and learn what their culture means to them.

The Problem Is Us

One of the most telling signs that we have problems engaging others across cultures in our country today is the fact that we don't recognize our complicity in cultural stereotyping. In almost any discussion of cultural representation, you'll find disagreement over what constitutes a stereotype, who is perpetuating them, and who has the right to claim they have suffered from being stereotyped. Most people think of a cultural stereotype as an overt physical or verbal insult against a person of another culture, like calling someone the "N-word" or a "wetback," making physical gestures that link a person with an animal, pulling your eyelids sidewise to look

East Asian, or creating pictorial associations with lynching and slavery. There is no doubt that all of these actions are despicable and should be condemned. But it's not enough for us to focus on these overt examples of stereotyping alone.

I'd like to propose a different definition of cultural stereotyping—namely, an oversimplified *story* about a person or group of people based on generalizations, limited interactions, and hearsay. I use this definition because people will often say they aren't racist toward other cultures or ethnicities, but when they are pressed further, they may still believe *stories* they've learned about groups of people that are reductive and hurtful. We can have imagined narratives about people of different skin colors or people who immigrate to our country, and these stories influence us in ways we may not realize. That's why this definition of cultural stereotyping is important. It acknowledges that stereotyping a person begins in how we think, often unconsciously. We formulate certain mindsets for or against another person, and then we treat them accordingly.

To some extent, cultural stereotyping is our way of trying to make sense of a new person. We think that categorizing and explaining people will help us better understand how to interact with them. But the problem is that we take shortcuts. Instead of embracing the complexity of an individual person, we ignore their diverse and detailed information and reduce them to a one-dimensional label, a stock character in a fictional story.

Embracing people as full-bodied humans, each unique in their own way, would mean having to process repeated information overloads. Learning the history, personality, beliefs, and preferences of every single person we meet takes significant time. It requires mental energy, and quite frankly, it's a lot of work, and most of us don't want to work that hard. So when there's too much information, the most adaptive response is to simplify by filtering out or ignoring the details and categorizing people into groups.[1] Instead of doing the hard work of getting to know someone as the unique person they are, we save energy by creating a simplistic image of that person based on a selection of their identifying features, including skin color and ethnicity. But this image will inevitably be fake. Even worse, stereotyping leads to racial bias. Our implicit assumptions about a person cause us to then place value judgments on them. They become either good or bad, safe or scary in our minds. For example, if we believe the narrative to fear Black and Brown bodies, then we may develop a strong negative reaction—a kind of fight or flight response—when we see a Black or Brown body in certain contexts.

The conversation on cultural stereotyping must begin with our mental processes, because beliefs lead to actions. If we only understand cultural stereotyping as overt physical or verbal gestures that denigrate someone, we will inaccurately reduce this issue to a list of things not to do or say. These are the surface-level problems, but there are deeper roots beneath these actions.

It's easy to spot the people who are blatantly insensitive to people of other cultures. They think it's funny to wear sombreros and fake mustaches on Mexican holidays or dress up like gangsters and post pictures of themselves in white undershirts on the internet. These are often the same people who consciously or unconsciously think that all immigrants are criminals or that all Muslims are terrorists. But if we think those are the only people who need to change, the future of cross-cultural relationships looks grim.

This book is for all of us, including well-meaning Christians who want to be more sensitive to the impact of their words and actions. Even those of us who are passionate about solidarity and who care about racial justice and diversity can still perpetuate cultural stereotypes, albeit in subtler ways. The truth is, even if you never act out an obscene gesture or say something overtly racist, you can still fail to see and treat people as individuals. As sociologist Nancy Wang Yuen says, "We [must] all acknowledge that . . . none of us are exempt from having racial biases."[2]

You may not verbalize to others the thought that Asian immigrants who speak broken English are dumb, but have you ever considered inviting an immigrant to your leadership table? You might never express the idea that Black women aren't beautiful, but have you ever had any interest in dating a woman with dark skin? You might not admit that you question how many Mexican Americans are here legally, but how often does the thought cross your mind when you see a Mexican construction worker or cook in a restaurant? Perhaps you're offended when people make comments about minority communities being "dangerous," but you yourself never go to their neighborhoods or shop in their grocery stores or visit their playgrounds. You might not come out and say you believe minorities are cheating the school system because of affirmative action, but whenever you meet a student of color, you secretly wonder how smart they are.

Thoughts like this can subtly creep into the fabric of our lives and color our relationships with others. The stereotypes we hold—whether we are aware of them or not—affect every relationship we have. They influence the way we choose our friends, our churches, and the people we associate with. They drive our decisions about which leaders we listen to and where we send our children to school. And they lead to problems like tokenism in organizations and leadership roles because we treat individual people of a particular ethnic group or skin color as representative of an entire cultural group instead of who they really are: unique human beings.

How we define cultural stereotypes also impacts the kinds of solutions we deem necessary moving forward. If we can begin to see cultural stereotyping as a mindset and as a process by which we filter *out* information about a person and reduce them to a label we can manage, then we can start holding the mirror up to ourselves. We are all part of the problem. We need to do better, and we can do better. If we are serious about change—real change that leads to understanding, healing, and conciliation across cultural lines—we first need to understand how our own brains need to change.[3] We need to *want* to humble ourselves, take time to self-reflect, and understand how we are failing to see people as they are.

See the Cultural Mosaic

The way to move forward is by *choosing to never see two people as exactly the same*. This is the challenge that Paul puts before us in 1 Corinthians 9:19–23 when he shares his model of cross-cultural engagement. In verses 20–21 he writes, "To the Jews I became like a Jew, to win the Jews. To those under the law I became like one not having the law (though I myself am not under the law), so as to win those under the law. To those not having the law I became like one not having the law (though I am not free from God's law but am under Christ's law)." Here Paul focuses on culturally adapting to the people around him, and implicit in his statement is the belief that each individual Jew and Gentile (i.e., those not having the law) is distinct and unique. When Paul, who is himself an ethnic Jew, says that he needs to become *like* a Jew, he is implying that not all Jews are the same nor should they be treated in the same way. Sensitivity and humility are required so that he can see both the differences and similarities between himself and people of his own ethnicity and then learn how to adapt accordingly. The same is true for Gentiles. No two Gentiles are the same, and Paul's goal is to learn how to connect with as many of them as possible.

Paul's implications on the distinctions of Jews and Gentiles in 1 Corinthians 9 force us to first readdress the people in the New Testament world. Traditionally, biblical scholarship has tended to overlook much of the ethnic diversity present in the first century.[4] Too often, it's assumed that when New Testament writers like Paul discuss Jews and Gentiles, they are referring to two monolithic ethnic groups. Occasionally, "barbarians" are included as a third group,[5] but there remains an underlying assumption that everyone who is not Jewish or barbarian is a Gentile (i.e., Greco-Roman). This couldn't be further from the truth, and it's certainly not how Paul viewed people in the first-century world. When Paul writes in 1 Corinthians 9:19–23 about Jews and Greco-Roman Gentiles, he's referring to a vast array of people groups.

The Jews of the first century, for example, were comprised of diverse nationalities, socioeconomic statuses, and political orientations. Many of the Jewish people we meet in the Scriptures include those living within Roman-occupied Palestine, such as the Pharisees, the Sadducees, the Zealots, and the people of the land (in Hebrew, *am ha'aretz*). In addition, there are the Samaritans, a people group distantly associated with the Jews. There are also those outside of Palestine who form the Jewish Diaspora and encompass different languages and even a certain degree of intermarriage, forming all sorts of hybrid cultural identities.

Paul identifies himself as "a Pharisee, descended from Pharisees" (Acts 23:6), educated at the feet of Gamaliel, the leading Pharisee of his day.[6] So when he says, "To the Jews I became like a Jew," he's saying that to reach every Jew—among the diversity present within the Judaism of his day—he must learn how to be something other than an educated Pharisee. Not every Jew is like Paul in the things they value and the ways they think, and connecting with each of them requires a different approach. He has to learn and adapt to the cultural narratives, expressions, and personalities of the differing Jewish groups, which requires overcoming long-standing obstacles between them. The Sadducees, for example, saw the Pharisees as their principal theological opponents. These groups held different opinions on the resurrection and the afterlife. The Sadducees maintained the "old-time religion" and looked down on the Pharisees as dangerous innovators—modernists, in fact.[7] For Paul to engage with the Sadducees *like* a Sadducee would mean seeking to dissolve tension and pursue peace with people who had probably been unkind to him in the past and vice versa. We see Paul conscious of his words, for example, in Acts 23:6–8 when he speaks to a crowd of both Pharisees and Sadducees. He carefully discerns when Sadducees are in his midst and learns how to converse on subjects he doesn't agree with, so that he can do so as an "insider," as one who really understands where the Sadducees are coming from, instead of simply criticizing and rejecting their ideas.

The Greeks Paul refers to are also incredibly diverse. Although the educated population of the Roman Empire tended to refer to themselves as Greeks, in reality they were made up of dozens of different Indo-European, Asian, and African ethnic groups.[8] The term *Greek* simply refers to anyone who is not a Jew, and in the first-century world that meant a whole lot of different people. Professor J. Daniel Hays points out that Acts 2 refers to the languages of Parthians, Medes, Elamites, Cretans, and Arabs as well as the languages spoken by the residents of Mesopotamia, Cappadocia, Pontus, Asia, Phrygia, Pamphylia, Egypt, and Cyrene.[9] All of these people groups had distinct identities, cultural narratives, languages, and religions. Similarly, the city of Corinth, where Paul wrote 1 Corinthians, was a booming cosmopolitan city. By the time Paul arrived there, around AD 50/51, Corinth was emerging as Greece's premier city and the commercial, manufacturing, and cultural megacenter of the entire eastern Mediterranean.[10] One would find a confluence of diverse people groups here as well, including black Africans from Meroe (in Greek, Ethiopians) and Berbers from North Africa.

So when Paul says in 1 Corinthians 9:21 that he has become *like* those not having the law, he is making a provocative claim that he has sought to become like each and every non-Jewish person he has come into contact with—whether Egyptian, African, Berber, or Syrian. He doesn't treat people as homogenized cultural groups. Each person's specific history, age, gender, geographical context (e.g., coastal/inland, urban/rural, regional/country), family, religious beliefs, professional occupation, socioeconomic status, and political affiliation makes them unique, even within their ethnic group, and appreciating a person's cultural makeup is the first step in pursuing healthy and appropriate cross-cultural relationships.

If this was how Paul viewed people and engaged with people in the first century, his approach should be all the more relevant for us today in our increasingly boundaryless world where no whole people group can be attributed to a "home country" or a particular type of food, tradition, dress, or physical appearance. Every individual is unique, and while individuals share certain common values with other people of a similar ethnic heritage, no two people are ever exactly the same.

The rubric in 1 Corinthians 9:19–23 is that culture is created at an individual level. Each individual is like *every other* human being, like *some other* human beings, and like *no other* human being. We all carry different layers of culture within ourselves, and we can trace the ways that our childhood, geographical location, educational background, personality, technological engagement, family, travels, and even our unique moment in history have influenced who we are. No one is monocultural. No two Asian Americans are the same. No two Latinos are the same. No two African Americans are the same. No two Native Americans are the same. No two Anglo Americans are the same either. Each of us is a cultural mosaic, consisting of our own unique combination of cultural tiles and patterns.[11] Each of us has a unique culture, story, and values that form who we are as a person.

This has been true in my life. I am like every Indian, like some Indians, and like no other Indian. As a bicultural, second-generation Indian American woman who grew up in Minnesota but now lives in Austin, Texas, I have pieces of both the Midwest and the South in me. My own identity includes the story of my mother's upbringing in Africa and my father's British and German heritage, a past that can be traced back to the daughters of the American Revolution. My narrative has both pride and pain. It includes stories of immigration and crossing borders—the journey of my mother's forefathers as forced laborers from India who built the British railroad and escaped from genocide under the rule of President Idi Amin, as well as my father's ancestors' journey as pilgrims on the *Mayflower*. My father's family are farmers, still deeply connected to the land, and are, in the best possible sense, stubborn, resilient, and tough. Each of these qualities was instilled in me at a very young age—just as much as the Indian values of respect for authority and an open-door approach to hospitality.

You'd be hard pressed to put me in a category. And that is true for you too. I don't know what your ethnic background is as you read this. Perhaps you identify with a particular ethnic group. Maybe you don't. Or perhaps you identify with more than one. Regardless, your story is uniquely you and like no other, and there is a danger in forcing our unique stories to fit into preconceived narratives. For example, Asian Americans are often seen as a wedge within the black-white divide, and people assume that most of us are simply "white adjacent." We're stereotyped as the model minority and as "crazy rich Asians," as if we are all wealthy and successful and live our lives like white people. However, not all Asians are rich. Asian Americans actually have the greatest income inequality and socioeconomic disparity of any racial demographic.[12] There are many poor Asians and Asian immigrants in our country. Consider also the assumptions about Indians in the United States. We're often reduced to a single representation within entertainment, usually as a comedic sidekick, and associated with IT outsourcing, motels, and convenience stores. That assumption, however, is based on many misunderstandings.

Yes, I grew up eating rice and dal. I wasn't allowed to talk to boys or to do much without my parents' permission. Weekends were for homework. I could never talk back to my mom and dad, and my family was involved in every aspect of my life. Many of my Indian friends had similar experiences growing up because much of Indian culture is driven by honor for our elders and duty to the family. Yet parts of me don't fit the Indian stereotype. I have light brown skin, and I don't speak Hindi (or Gujarati) fluently. I don't attend an all-Indian church. I'm not particularly tech-savvy. I like to be punctual, and I prefer eating dinner before 9:00 p.m. Though my mother is a Patel, our family has never owned a convenience store. I speak German and love literature. I'm a professor, an author, an Enneagram 8, and an activist. I'm married to a Mexican American. We're church planters in Austin, Texas, who also happen to enjoy barbecue and watching football. No other person is quite like me. No one is quite like you either.

Seeing an individual's culture as a cultural mosaic challenges us to look at the many pieces that form a person. He or she may have some tiles that identify them with a particular national or ethnic group while also sharing tiles—points of commonality—with a wide range of peoples, cultures, and traditions. If we should engage people the way Paul did, we need to focus on the uniqueness of each person.

A New Way Forward

Everyone wants to be understood for who they are, including their complexities and what makes them unique. Everyone has a past and hopes for the future. We have joys, pains, and stories to tell. Each of us is on a journey of becoming. We're not who we used to be, and we won't be the exact same person we are now in the years to come. Our challenge is to apply how we want to be known and seen—as unique individuals—so that we see all people in this way. Here are a few suggestions that will help us do this.

Never Treat Someone as Representative of an Entire Ethnic Group

First, stop making assumptions about people based on what you think you know. Period. Don't assume all Black people are entertainers or athletes. If a person of color tells you they went to college, don't ask what sport they played (or act surprised that they went to college). Like anyone else, Black and Brown people should be able to pursue any kind of hobby, interest, or skill without being told, "I didn't know people like you did that." Don't assume all Latinos speak Spanish or all Asians speak broken English. Many of us were raised with English as our first language. Not all Asians are good at math or are tiger parents, bad drivers, or cheap customers. Don't assume Latinos have low-income jobs and are lazy. Don't believe the myth that all Native Americans are impoverished, live on reservations, operate casinos, and are completely immersed in traditional Indigenous culture. Their stories, experiences, passions, and pursuits are as complex as those of any other cultural group. Don't think that the lone Black man walking down the street is up to no good or that Black or Brown people hanging out at a street corner are dangerous. Similarly, don't assume that all Muslims are terrorists or that every white person is insensitive to issues of poverty and racism. There is no justification ever for us to make assumptions about what kinds of food a person prefers, what mindset they have, whether or not they fit in with or belong to an ethnic group, where they're from, how rich or poor they are, how they should talk and act, or what kind of job they should have. All of these assumptions are barriers to developing strong cross-cultural relationships with others.

Remember, a stereotype by definition is seeing everyone who belongs to a particular cultural group as similar—it's a mental picture of every person of a certain ethnicity having predefined traits. But asking one Puerto Rican woman to represent Latinas *everywhere* is an impossible task. It is equally wrong when we treat one Black man as the standard for African American men or one Korean American woman as a model for all Asian American women. We need to stop saying things like "all white people," "all Black people," "all Asians," or "all Latinos." Don't buy into the lie that a grain of truth lies beneath every stereotype. There is no such thing as a stereotypical Indian man or woman. There is no such thing as the "model minority," or any other stereotype for that matter.[13] That's the first lie that needs to go. I could never speak for all Indians, and I certainly hope that others don't assume all Indians are just like me. I have Indian friends in California, Alabama, and Mumbai, and they are all different people. I don't look like anyone else. I don't dress like anyone else. I don't think like anyone else. I am not a spokesperson for all Indians everywhere. My opinions are my own.

Moreover, when we interact with people based on stereotypes, we create breeding grounds for tokenism—the practice of symbolic efforts for diversity. Too often, a single (or a few) people of color are recruited to give the appearance of ethnic and cultural equality within a workplace. However, the problem is that having a token person of color satisfies the quota for a certain level of diversity, and no further actions are taken to change the power dynamics or improve the inclusion policies in an organization. For example, when we think that a single Asian American is representative of all Asians, we won't feel the need to hire more than one Asian on our task force. We won't see or value diversity within an ethnic group because we think they are all the same. The most extreme version of tokenism I have ever experienced was when I was treated as interchangeable with an African American woman. My voice wasn't needed in that particular company, or so I was told, because they already had a woman of color on staff. We usually don't think that a white person would be able to fairly represent all white people. Have you ever heard a company tell a white person, "Sorry, we can't hire you because we already have another white person on staff"? We should never place these same types of restrictions on Black and Brown people either.

Give People the Honor of Self-Definition

We also need to give greater weight to and be careful about the names we use to describe cultural groups. Research now shows that receiving a name is a form of "social tagging," as every name comes with associated expectations regarding characteristics, behaviors, and even a stereotypical "look" within a culture.[14] In other words, what you call someone directly impacts how you view them. The most honoring thing we can do for a person of another culture is to give them the dignity of defining themselves. This practice takes the power and ability to place value judgments on others out of our hands and challenges us to see someone the way they want to be seen, not according to how we want to label them.

This is especially important today, as we have a wide

variety of terms that people use within our society as a whole. Should you say Native American or First Nation peoples? East Indian, South Asian, or Desi? Chicano, Latino, or Latin American? Black, African American, African, or Afro-Latino? The fact that we have this wealth of terms reflects the diversities of peoples and their preferences for different self-identifications.

Many of us have families in different countries. This is particularly true for individuals with bicultural and multicultural identities. Our ethnic heritages are mixed. For example, I have both Indian and British/German heritage. I have friends who are part Black and part Asian or part Asian and part Latino and many other combinations in between. We are often misidentified because of our mixed traits. It's important that people never assume that someone's phenotype is a direct giveaway of their ethnicity. Though I may have lighter skin than some other Indians, I resonate with my Indian cultural identity more than my European heritage—partly because of the traditions and foods that formed me while growing up, but also because people have always treated me as a brown-skinned minority woman. Every person defines their cultural identity differently based on the narratives they resonate with most.

Many first-generation immigrants in the United States identify with their country of origin. They refer to themselves simply as El Salvadorian, Burmese, Colombian, Dominican, or Chinese. Second- and third-generation immigrants and beyond, on the other hand, often begin to claim more racialized American categories like Latino, Asian American, or

Black. We understand the way race in America works, and we change our identification to reflect that. Our identity is, nevertheless, still quite diverse.

This is why it's still important to understand the distinctions between terms like *Latino, Hispanic,* and *Latinx*. They're often used interchangeably to describe a group that makes up about 18 percent of the US population and with ties to over twenty different Latin American countries. The term *Hispanic* was created in a census by the US government in 1980.[15] It's not a term that Spanish-speakers created for themselves, which is why my husband, for example, always prefers to be called Mexican American and never Hispanic. At the same time, many persons of Mexican descent reject the term *Mexican American* as something imposed on them and call themselves Chicanos instead. There are complicated histories at work here, and each person engages with these histories differently. The same is true for the term *Black*. An Afro-Colombian may prefer to never be called Black, while a quarter of all Latinos in the United States self-identify as Afro-Latino, Afro-Caribbean, or of African descent with roots in Latin America.[16] Speaking of terms, *Asian American* was a label created by Asian American activists and organizers in the late '60s and early '70s as a way to disassociate from the white American imposed term *oriental*, and many today embrace *Asian American* as a positive and empowering form of identification. But never forget that the Asian American population in the United States is estimated to be between twenty and twenty-two million. We represent forty-eight different countries in Asia as well as an Asian diaspora around the world, speaking hundreds of languages collectively. We are distinct and diverse. No matter who you are trying to connect with, always be as local and specific as you can.

Remember: what is true for one person may not be true for another. Every single person will prefer a different term that reflects their specific cultural narrative. The best thing to do is ask. Then honor that person by using the term they use, regardless of whether it fits with your preprogrammed categories.

Focus on an Individual's Cultural Narrative

Our continual emphasis on "facts" about a particular ethnicity or generic cultural information over personal narratives can create immediate barriers in cross-cultural relationships. People don't bond over generic cultural facts. I don't feel connected to someone just because they've watched *Slumdog Millionaire*. That's great, and I'm glad they've watched the movie, but that's not my story, and I don't want my life compared to the protagonist in that fictional world. I don't mind being asked what I *thought* about a certain Bollywood film and whether I liked it (I do enjoy watching Bollywood films after all). But if someone really wants to get to know me, I'd rather they ask me about the meaningful things happening in my life, things that are unique to me, my journey, and my view of the world.

When we meet someone from a different culture, our aim should be to get to know them as an individual and learn what is unique about them. We should want to talk about the things that are important to them, to see life through their eyes, and to make them feel heard, validated, and loved. Don't make assumptions about what a person likes or dislikes. Be cautious of labeling everything as a by-product of white privilege, white supremacy, and patriarchy. Don't ask leading questions like "Where are you from?" or say things like "If Asians can get out of poverty, then Latinos can too," or "You're different, not like other Black people I know." These kinds of statements are always painful, whether the other person reveals that to you or not. Instead, ask open-ended questions like "What's your story?" "What are you passionate about?" and "What are your roots?" Then just listen. Enjoy the person for who he or she is instead of trying to compare and categorize them into a fictional group.

No matter who we are engaging with, we need to challenge ourselves to learn more, to dig deeper, and to see individuals for who they are. We must have the willingness, as author MelindaJoy Mingo writes, "to see every human being from God's perspective and not through the lens of prejudices, stereotypes, and negative societal influences."[17] So ask yourself: What stereotypes have I constructed about other cultural groups, and who am I avoiding as a result? How might my perception of someone from a different culture be lacking? What parts of their personhood have I filtered out? What racial biases do I have, and how can I work to deconstruct them? How can I get to know a person better? What is unique about him or her?

Cross-cultural engagement is all about how *we* need to change, and the rest of the book attempts to explore that idea chapter by chapter. Now that we know we *need* to change, let's get to work.

Chapter 3

Embrace Cultural Discomfort

During grad school, my favorite place to write was a multipurpose lounge on campus. People rarely came in because the booths were old and the lighting was dingy, but for me this unused space was a treasure trove of solitude. I got some of my best work done in that lounge. Occasionally a fellow doctoral student would trickle in, but they never made a sound, and we all felt like we shared a secret in coming to this place. That's the thing about our preferences: like tends to congregate with like, and it creates a sense of belonging.

I had been coming here for months and had never been interrupted—not once! But then, one day, everything changed.

That afternoon, as I was reading Foucault's *Technologies of the Self* for what felt like endless hours, and my eyes were beginning to glaze over, the door to the tiny lounge suddenly burst open, and a sea of noise came rushing in. A group of ten Korean men speaking loudly walked up to the biggest table in the middle of the room and began assembling a communal meal. Lunch boxes and Tupperware began magically appearing out of backpacks, and eventually the whole table was covered with a veritable feast. In the course of a few minutes our quiet room began to echo loudly with the sounds of smacking and slurping. The feelings of discomfort experienced by the others in the room were palpable.

Granted, I'm not threatened by noise. For the most part, Indians are at home in loud environments. Parties and holiday gatherings never seem complete until the house is jammed full of people, food, music, and laughter. Kids run around, shouting and doing who-knows-what, while moms and aunties cook amazing things in the kitchen and talk loudly. That's just what we do in our culture: we eat and we talk, and then we eat some more. Get-togethers are loud. People are everywhere and everyone's happy. You could say that happiness in Indian culture is displayed with a high-decibel accompaniment.

Korean culture, from what I've learned from my Korean American friends, shares a good deal of overlap with Indian culture in this regard. So, while the abrupt introduction of noise into our quiet study lounge felt a bit jarring (I had wanted to get some work done, after all), I didn't mind it too much.

There were two other students in the room, however, both of whom were white, who were more than just a little annoyed by the change. To them, these men were intruders who had committed a grave offense.

Noise is one of those things that often creates a divide between people of dominant and subdominant cultures. Watch any movie about cross-cultural relations, and the "problem" of noise will become immediately apparent. Typically, white folks feel overwhelmed by how loud their culturally different neighbors, coworkers, or potential in-laws are.

The Korean men weren't doing anything wrong. We were in a public space, and they had every right to eat there and talk as loudly as they wanted to. The lounge had no specific rules about noise. What they were doing wasn't the norm for that space, but it wasn't breaking any rules either. Still, the decibel at which they were speaking extended well beyond my two fellow students' comfort levels and had clearly upset them.

It doesn't matter what your skin color or ethnicity is, we can all feel this way under certain circumstances. When your neighbors blare music in their backyard during a party, when that tenant in the apartment above you is making "too much noise" and you're trying to sleep, when that person in the pew next to you at church is singing too loud, when someone sounds like they're practically shouting on their phone while sitting at the bus stop or listening to music without headphones, or when someone is making noise outside your baby's window during nap hours, our response isn't as simple as "Well, that's different, but I guess I'll get used to it." I wish we were all that easygoing. Most of the time we become angry, walk out our front door, and give looks, make comments, and possibly even file a complaint or call the police. That's what we do when somebody disrupts our comfort and intrudes into "our" space.

And that's exactly what happened in that dingy old study lounge that day. The two students became visibly upset, sending exaggerated glares at the group of Korean men. You know the look you try to give people when you are upset with them and you hope they will immediately understand how you feel from the sternness on your face? Well, that's what they were doing, and it wasn't working. Their comfortable space had been disrupted with layers of discomfort, and if menacing stares would not restore things to the way they were, they were ready to take their communication to the next level.

I watched in horror as one of the white women stood up and confidently marched over to the table of Korean men. It was like a scene from a movie where you know the person is going to push the wrong button and everything is about to explode, but it was too late to stop it from happening. Disaster was imminent.

"Excuse me," she shouted, standing authoritatively over them with her hands on her hips, "You guys need to quiet down, or I'm going to have to ask you to leave."

Her words felt like a bomb going off.

Even though I wasn't the insulted party, I immediately felt their shame. It was the shame of being Asian American and only being treated well if you live up to the myth of the silent, model minority, the shame of white culture placing rules and restrictions on how Brown bodies should talk, laugh, eat, act, and be. Our society has created labels to describe these behaviors like "the loud Black woman" or "the quiet Asian" to enforce a white default for appropriate expressions and volumes, and these stereotypes use noise levels to create parameters of success or failure for minorities.

That's what makes situations like this one so complicated. It's wrapped up in power dynamics lurking beneath the surface. The white woman's expectation, of which perhaps she was unaware, was that these Koreans would do exactly as she requested. This was a power play with threats leveled to enforce her preferred standard. Whether she realized it or not, she was expressing her own personally mediated racism in coded language, using her position of privilege to get what she wanted. This sort of behavior is not at all uncommon, happening far more often than we'd like to admit.

By now, we're all familiar with the narrative of cops being called because of a potential disturbance caused by a Black man or a group of Brown people. Privilege is weaponized to impose a cultural imperialism against those who do not follow the majority cultural protocols. We demand that someone else adhere to our norms, believing that our cultural standards are better than theirs. We come in with what we feel is the right volume (or words, or behavior, or music, or dress code) for our community and try to hang that over someone else's head, instead of learning how to be culturally flexible.

The question of noise level is just one example. Each of our preferences for certain standards of living is predicated on personal cultural values, and our unwillingness to adapt to and be flexible with other expressions, volumes, and tones is a big factor in the sort of oil-and-water relationships that we have across cultures today. It's not easy to adapt or mix the two when one or both see themselves as right and the other as wrong.

How Much Can You Put Up With?

Listen, I know it's hard to embrace someone else's cultural values. Whether it's their noise level, the smell and look of their food, their communal gatherings, or the way they look at you, talk, dress, or act, another person's way of life often feels like a disruption. Their actions and words can annoy us or make us feel uncomfortable, and more often than not our response is to avoid the person, the situation, or both. But this kind of cultural inflexibility can cause real damage. Friendships are lost, trauma is inflicted, lives are marginalized, even lost. The stakes are high.

I know you are reading this because you already recognize that a corrective is in order. Most of us would agree that we don't want to live in a world of white privilege, a world where white culture is the invisible default determining what is acceptable and unacceptable in society. We say that we value diversity and human flourishing, but being unwilling to embrace or appreciate other people's cultural identities— their ethnicity and their unique story—in our community, workforce, place of worship, or even our own family will only perpetuate and reinforce this invisible default standard.[1]

When we choose to confront cultural differences with more rules, we fall into the trap of cultural policing. Natural hair types are scrutinized and legislated by unwritten (or sometimes written) American policies. African American women are called unprofessional or even refused job appointments if they don't conform to the straight-hair standard. There are demands that minorities and immigrants only speak English and that "formal English" should be spoken instead of slang, Ebonics, and other variations of the English language. People refuse to go to someone's house because it "smells," or they tell their housemate what foods she can or cannot cook in their apartment so the place won't reek of spices. There's a low tolerance for things like head scarves, turbans, and other "foreign" clothing items. Brown-skinned people are asked—in their own neighborhoods—if they live there. Neighbors make complaints that the family next door has too many people in a house, or that their guests are "clogging up" the street. Cultural differences make us uncomfortable so we decide they are wrong and must be stopped.

Different cultures coming together will always create tension. We value different things, and we express our values differently too. But a fear of other people's cultures causes real and detrimental effects. As long as we see someone else's way of life as inappropriate or wrong, we will focus our energy on controlling how the other person talks, walks, laughs, thinks, and behaves. The more we dislike what someone else is doing, the more we will define our society and the spaces we inhabit by notions of superiority and isolationism rather than tolerance, acceptance, and openness. The resistance to cultural change, even change to cultural values, is part of an effort to control our country's social fabric through the exclusion and intimidation of people outside the center. That is something Christians should resist, as it is the antithesis to biblical notions of racial solidarity where people of all cultures and ethnicities are to be welcomed and celebrated for who they are. Resistance to cultural change, in contrast, is the gateway to xenophobia, racism, and nativism.

Loving our neighbors means learning to love people different than we are. We need to become comfortable with alternative ways of doing things and ask ourselves, "How much cultural discomfort am I willing to bear?" We will not even know how to answer this question unless we are willing to sit in our own discomfort and begin listening to and appreciating our fellow human beings.

It's Not Right or Wrong, Just Different

The first step to becoming more culturally flexible is as simple as this: the next time someone of another culture does something that makes you feel uncomfortable, *don't immediately jump to the conclusion that they are wrong.* Jewish Christians were doing exactly this in the first-century church. In the book of Acts, we read about Jewish Christians who traveled to Antioch and demanded that the Gentile Christians there be circumcised and follow the Mosaic law. These Jewish believers were essentially saying to their non-Jewish brothers and sisters, "If you want us to accept you, you need to become like us. To live your life any other way is wrong." By the time Paul, Barnabas, and the elders learn of this, they know a correction is needed. In Acts 15, a council convenes in Jerusalem, and the apostles challenge the Christian leaders gathered there to stop demanding that Gentiles become Jewish to be considered part of the family of God. Rather, in this new age—the church age—the Spirit of God meets people where they are and transformation will be from the inside out. Christians' demands for outward cultural conformity must come to an end.

The demand for conformity is one of the big differences between the Mosaic covenant of the Old Testament and the new covenant of the New Testament. The former required people to become like the Israelites both theologically *and* culturally. It involved numerous outward marks, like circumcision, that physically defined what it meant to be an Israelite and part of God's people. But under the new covenant, the gospel redeems all people and cultures. God no longer asks us all to adapt to one particular culture but instead asks us to become like the people we seek to reach. We need to have greater cultural flexibility and should avoid a strict right-wrong mentality when we encounter different cultural expressions. No matter how uncomfortable we might feel, we Christians must remind ourselves that some things are not right or wrong; they are just different. When people of different ethnicities and cultural narratives come together, the differences will always be palpable. But instead of trying to mute or control those differences, we should accommodate ourselves to other people's cultures. Under the new law, we don't demand that people change who they are. We change ourselves for them.

This is the theology of cultural accommodation in a nutshell.[2]

The alternative is monocultural Christianity. Yet nowhere under the new covenant do we see Christians required to all act the same way. New covenant Christianity allows for diverse cultural expressions of a common faith. Moreover, unlike the ethnic and civil laws of the old covenant, the new covenant encourages us to become malleable and flexible to adapt to the uniqueness of each individual situation. For example, Paul expects different things from both Timothy and Titus. He tells Timothy to become circumcised because he is working among Jews and his mother is a Jew (Acts 16:1), while Titus, a Greek, can remain uncircumcised (Gal. 2:3–5). Every person in every context now demands a different approach.

The idea of cultural adaptability remains a controversial topic among Christians. It requires a certain allowance for cultural relativism, and we fear that this approach will threaten the permanence of biblical truths.[3] However, understood correctly, changing both our perceptions (what we think) and actions (what we do) from one cultural context to the next should not pose a conflict for Christians. Rightly understood and practiced, cultural accommodation affirms deeply held biblical principles and truths. We hold Christian ethics and morality in one hand, in continuity with Christians of the past, while extending the other hand to people of other cultures as we desire to understand them and share the truth about God with them in their own unique way.

The gospel and our faith must be contextualized from one person to the next. This is not just a suggestion; it's a warning. Because when we choose not to change for the people around us, we end up creating unhealthy rubrics for what constitutes appropriate and inappropriate cultural expressions for followers of Jesus. And this choice leads to irrevocable pain and trauma for people. That's what's at stake here. A failure on our part to accommodate to the cultures around us means we risk the danger of perpetuating ethnocentrism and racial hierarchies and, ultimately, turning people away from Christ.

We can stop this cycle. Paul provides a clue for how in 1 Corinthians 9:22 when he writes that we should become all things to all people. Consider his ministry among Jewish converts as well as Jewish people who had not yet come to faith. With them, he is prepared to follow Jewish customs. Implicit in Paul's worldview is a refusal to construct dichotomies of insiders and outsiders.[4] There is no hint of hierarchy, no hint of Paul seeing himself as better than the people around him or serving them as if he was their savior instead of Jesus. Paul's actions imply a view of himself as a relative nobody. He treats himself as if he is the one on the margins, the one without power, as a way to care for everyone.

Practically, this means he's prepared to change what he eats, how he prays, and how he dresses. This commitment even leads Paul to shave his head before leaving Corinth. In Acts 18:18 we read, "Paul stayed on in Corinth for some time. Then he left the brothers and sisters and sailed for Syria, accompanied by Priscilla and Aquila. Before he sailed, he had his hair cut off at Cenchreae because of a vow he had taken." After approximately two years in Corinth, Paul heads back to Jerusalem to meet with professing Jews, who call upon him to take a Nazirite vow. Though Paul is under no obligation to take this vow, he does so because he knows it will help prevent any stumbling blocks to his presentation of the gospel among them.

Paul also sacrifices in the temple in Acts 21:17–26, which by all accounts doesn't make any sense. He knows that Christ has come and become the ultimate and final sacrifice for sin. Yet here he is, performing the practices of the old law to connect with Jewish Christians in Jerusalem. This is one of those scenes that makes your head explode! Paul is engaging in an activity that he would have considered irrelevant to his newfound faith in Jesus. But does he lecture these Jewish Christians and tell them they are wrong? Does he act like he's better than they are? No. He puts the interests of others above his own because he knows there is a relational cost to resistance with little to be gained.

The choices Paul makes—performing religious activities that he didn't personally believe in, shaving his head, and eating foods outside of his traditional upbringing—aren't small things. They are bold measures, actions that came at a cost and at the very least would make many of us uncomfortable. However, if Paul was willing to do this, we have to ask ourselves if we are willing to culturally accommodate ourselves for the sake of others as well. Would you change the way you worship, what you eat, something about your physical appearance, or your way of life to connect with someone of a different culture? Could you learn to tolerate a new level of noise or the way someone is conducting themselves in a public space, choosing to keep that critique stuck in your throat instead of voicing it? Could you do that for each person of another culture that you meet?

What I'm talking about is not adopting the latest trend or trying to be alternative. The reason Paul neither holds on to his culture tightly nor fears cultural change is because it is more important for him to adapt for the sake of the gospel than to demand that people of other cultures become like him. The practice of cultural accommodation lowers the cultural barriers to the gospel by meeting people where they are, thereby enabling the maximum number of people to hear of Christ without giving them additional grounds to stumble.

Paul is constantly on the lookout for anything in his actions or life that needs to change in order to share the gospel more widely.

Of course, it's important to be clear what this does *not* mean. This is not about reducing Christ to a palatable mixture of love, kindness, and peace. The message of the Lord Jesus Christ, crucified and raised from the dead (1 Cor. 15:3–4), must not be changed. Even though becoming all things to all people requires a great deal of change on our part, we still need to measure whether our changes are being made for the sake of the gospel. Paul would never distort the gospel to accommodate cultural preferences. For example, he refuses to accommodate the message of the wisdom of Christ to the prevailing Greek understanding of wisdom (something the Corinthian church was trying to do). And like Paul we need to ask if Jesus would have adapted himself in the particular way we are considering. Jesus met a lot of people right where they were and crossed a lot of cultural boundaries that upset his fellow Jewish contemporaries. He was culturally flexible in more ways than we might realize. But if there was something he wouldn't do (because it did not reflect the character and will of God), we shouldn't either.

The challenge for us is discerning what is a nonnegotiable from what is difficult or burdensome. There were things Jesus did not want to do but still chose to do anyway. Think of his plea in the garden of Gethsemane, where he asks God to "take this cup from me" (Luke 22:42). Jesus did not want to suffer physical pain and torture or and die by crucifixion, but he embraced discomfort, pain, and even death for our sake.

Jesus came to serve, not to be served. We know from Luke 22:19–20 that when Jesus offered up his body on the cross and poured out his blood so that we might be forgiven of our sins, he was establishing the new covenant: "He took bread, gave thanks and broke it, and gave it to them, saying, 'This is my body given for you; do this in remembrance of me.' In the same way, after the supper he took the cup, saying, 'This cup is *the new covenant* in my blood, which is poured out for you'" (emphasis added). Jesus's life, death, and ministry are the premier example of a theology of cultural accommodation under the new covenant.

Being followers of Jesus means, at the very least, being willing to embrace discomfort in order to serve others. We need to consider how we may have excluded or turned away people of other cultures from the gospel because of our own rigidity and resistance to cultural change. There are many who might more readily give the gospel a proper hearing if they knew that we were willing to accommodate ourselves to them. We should not be afraid of people or fear the discomfort of personal change. Rather, we should be afraid of misrepresenting Jesus.

Let's Take This One Step at a Time

This is not going to be easy.

At times, no matter how much you repeat in your head some mantra, like "Be cool with this," you will still feel the tension and discomfort rising to levels you wish they wouldn't. You might even lose your nerve, perhaps more often than you'd like. In what I share with you, I want to be realistic, because *we never fully move past our cultural discomfort.* I wish I could tell you there was a formula that, once mastered, meant you'd never feel uncomfortable around a person of a different culture again. But it will inevitably happen, and it will keep happening until the Lord calls us home.

I'm simply here to help you lean into the discomfort instead of running away or trying to control the situation. Sometimes this means learning to keep your mouth shut, minding your own business, and forcing your body to do things you don't want to do. Even more, it's about learning to move beyond silent disengagement toward joy-filled engagement with others. Here are a few basic steps to becoming more comfortable in the discomfort and building connections across cultures instead of picking fights.

Stop and Take a Deep Breath

First, don't immediately blow up when someone says or does something you don't like. Don't scream or shout or verbally insult the other person. And don't walk away either. I can't even count the number of times I've seen a white person get angry with a person of color and show their disgust by both walking out *and* drawing attention to their exit. Don't do that. It's damaging.

Instead, when we get upset or uncomfortable because of something a person of another culture has said or done, we need to stop and consider: What is the underlying issue here? What's really making me mad right now? All too often, our immediate emotional outburst says more about us than it does about the other person. We first need to consider the ways we might be misjudging the person or the situation.

Stop and take a deep breath. You need to think about an appropriate response. You need a plan. You also need to pray. Give yourself the space and the time necessary to reflect and assess before responding (and also so you don't do something you'll later regret).

Remind Yourself: You Are Not the Standard

Second, we should never assume that who we are or how we do things is "normal." That's true for *any* person of *any* culture. When it comes to culture, we must remember that *every* person has an ethnicity and a story, and the way other people live isn't always a matter of right and wrong. Sometimes it's just different from the way you or I would do things. No one person or cultural group is the standard. No one person gets to place a higher value on his or her own cultural identity. Instead, we need to unlearn our assumptions about right and wrong cultural expressions and begin with the more neutral category of *different*.

Whether we realize it or not, American society is constructed with whiteness as its standard. In other words, how Americans view everything from noise levels and communication styles to dress codes, music preferences, and foods reflects what makes white people most comfortable. This is one reason that the minute you (if you are a white American) start to feel uncomfortable, you have to immediately remind yourself: I am not the standard. No matter our ethnic background, we must recognize what we consider normative and work to deconstruct our own inflexible parameters. I say this because people of color can be guilty of judging and making fun of white people and fellow people of color too. You don't want to be a barrier to diverse expressions of faith in Jesus.

People in the ethnic majority deserve to be treated with dignity and worth as fellow image bearers of God. Minorities need to have the freedom to be themselves, to return to their roots, and to express their stories. Not only that, but they should also be able to lead. Are you willing to hand over the reins of leadership to people of color so they can actively participate in the spaces you inhabit together? When people of color lead, honor them. Genuinely listen to them. Learn from them. Promote them. And give them an equal voice in creating the parameters of what is and isn't appropriate in any given context. People of color will never truly feel valued or appreciated until the power dynamics between dominant and subdominant cultures begin to change.

Equally important, people in subdominant cultures should not be penalized for their differences. And this is a word for both white people and people of color. If you stop hanging out with a person of a different ethnicity just because you don't like the way they do things, if you choose not to hire a woman of color because of her hairstyle or the outfit she wears to her interview, if you organize a special meeting to let a Black man in your church know you don't like the way he talks about white evangelicalism, if you condescend to a Latina and make her feel like she's being too emotional, if you constantly make jokes about the way an immigrant says things on account of his accent, then you are penalizing people for being who they are.

Even worse, seeking to control people like this can place real lives in danger. The minute we begin to justify silencing, forcibly detaining, and physically harming others because of their differences, we travel down the road of dehumanizing and demonizing entire people groups. Far too often, Black men are inaccurately stereotyped as criminals and threats, Latinos are seen as illegal, and Asians are treated as the bearers of deadly viruses. Thinking this way plants seeds that lead to controlling and sometimes even killing Black and Brown bodies.[5]

Choose to Delight in New Narratives

Third, each cultural difference is an expression of a different story, and our challenge is to learn from and delight in new narratives. This means seeing the beauty in your neighbor's communal celebration instead of seeing them as a noisy nuisance. Instead of thinking that a woman's hairstyle is ugly, look at her and see her as a child of God whose image is reflected in the uniqueness and beauty of her physical appearance. Instead of telling someone they need to learn English, learn to appreciate other people's native tongues and the powerful ways these languages communicate their cultural narratives. Instead of seeing foods from other cultures as disgusting because of their "strong odors" or different flavors and textures, find ways to appreciate the richness, creativity, and variety of other people's heritage. Seek to build bridges, not walls.

Instead of asking a neighbor, coworker, or even a stranger at the park to stop what they are doing—to be quiet, turn down their music, or leave—challenge yourself to enjoy that person and who they are in that moment. It can be as simple as smiling. Or you can walk over and introduce yourself. If you see someone in your neighborhood or at a park doing something you consider suspicious, don't immediately call the police. First, treat them as innocent until proven guilty. You'll have to entertain the idea that they might not be doing anything suspicious at all. You can also start praying and ask God to use this moment to work on your heart. Second, talk to the person. If you don't feel comfortable doing that alone, grab a friend, a neighbor, or your spouse to come with you. Go over with a posture of humility and a willingness to listen and learn instead of immediately accusing the person of a crime. Honestly, though, usually the best thing to do in situations like this is for each of us to mind our own business. If you're invited to someone's home for dinner and don't enjoy the food, still try to eat as much of it as you can without complaining. If you're in a meeting and are getting frustrated with a coworker's views on a subject, instead of immediately shooting down their ideas, listen deeply and consider how their culture and experiences are informing their ideas. Do the hard but necessary work of having real conversations with people and, instead of immediately accusing them of committing an offense, give them the honor of sharing things from their perspective. This is about leaning in and not pushing away, choosing to encourage, affirm, and embrace something that might feel unnatural, instead of trying to regulate, police, and restrict. To be all things to all people means showing Christ in ways that make sense to the other person, not in whatever way makes us most comfortable.

Ask yourself: What does love for this person look like in this moment?

Remember that people's lives convey stories, so getting to the heart of your cultural differences means learning to see and understand what narrative the other person is communicating. That perspective should keep us humble as we strive to see what life is like through another person's eyes. We must consider what is meaningful to them and how their stories in turn can become meaningful to us.

Lean into the Discomfort

Cultural accommodation will always be difficult because there will always be risks. You are stepping outside your comfort zone and making yourself vulnerable, and pain is not always avoidable. Letting go of our cultural preferences and embracing those of another is deeply personal and intimate. These are the things that define us—our identities and our uniquely personal expressions—and it will *always* be hard to be entirely flexible with these preferences. It will always be emotional on some level and filled with awkwardness and even failure, and if it's not, you are likely not stretching yourself far enough.

But this is a discomfort we must be willing to step into. If Paul was committed to cultural adaptability in the first-century world, how much more should we be ready to embrace it in our multicultural society today? We should practice cultural accommodation with every person we meet, whether they are a coworker, a neighbor, a person at church, the guy next to you at the café, a stranger walking down the street, or even a family member or spouse. Consider how you can accommodate your cultural preferences to better love and serve your classmates, your siblings, and the person sitting behind you on the train. Remember, cultural accommodation is for everyone.

If you are reading this as a white person, and especially if you've never had to cross into someone else's culture before, this probably won't be easy for you. You will need to be humble and practice giving up control. You will feel out of place, possibly for the first time in your life, and feel incredibly uncomfortable. Choose to sit in that discomfort and learn from it. Be willing to see and experience things not as right and wrong but as different.

People of color like me must recognize that we can be rigid in our own ways too. Asian Americans have preferred ways of doing things. African Americans, Latinos, Native Americans, South Africans, Middle Easterners, Native Hawaiians, and other Pacific Islanders all have standards, preferences, and opinions as well. Each of us finds it hard to imagine another culture having as rich a heritage of hospitality, food, and community as our own. It's not easy to embrace a white person's values when you've experienced their scorn. It's also hard to be culturally flexible with others when we're still on a journey of learning and celebrating our own culture. It's okay to go slow.

But don't give up. Keep challenging yourself not to judge your fellow white brothers and sisters. We can be critical without being condescending. Celebrate your culture and your people, while also making room for other communities of color to express themselves fully. Remember that you too are becoming all things to all people for a purpose. Choose to love and persevere. I promise, it's worth it.

Chapter 4

Rethink Code Switching, Privileges, and Rights

I'm sure you are familiar with the story of Cinderella. Maybe you have never read the original story with its powerful female protagonists and dark themes, but perhaps you've seen one of the movies. Truth be told, this was one of my favorite tales to teach in folklore courses when I was a German professor. It's a classic rags-to-riches tale, and the original message really has nothing to do with romance or falling in love. The story was written by and for peasants, and it acknowledges that they could never get out of poverty on their own. Their only hope for a better life was for a benefactor embodied by a fairy godmother to take pity on them, give them nice clothes and a new ride, and help them climb the social ladder.

One of the most notable scenes in the Disney film is when the fairy grandmother waves her wand, and Cinderella's pink rags magically transform into a blue ballroom gown. It's a profound moment that undergirds one of the basic messages of the tale: clothes make a person. There's even a psychological term for this idea called enclothed cognition.[1] It means we act in certain ways based on what we are wearing. When we dress up in a tuxedo or evening gown, for example, we will most likely behave differently than if we are at home in pajamas or in a running outfit. In the fairy tale, Cinderella dresses up so she can play a role. She wears clothes that allow her to "fit in." Cinderella wasn't born rich. She didn't understand that world. But she changed how she looked, how she talked, and how she behaved until she was accepted by the ruling elite. She acted like a princess, and then people started treating her like a princess.

The Cinderella tale is just as relatable today as it illustrates the story of many minorities who continue to change themselves to fit into majority society. No, not every Black and Brown person is poor, but many of us still try to fake it with our white friends until we make it. Many of us try to dress, act, and talk differently from our own cultural norms so we will be accepted in predominantly white environments. We pretend like we're white until we feel like we've succeeded with our white friends and coworkers.

I know because this used to be me.

My entire life, I've learned that acting white will get me further. If I talk, dress, and act the way white people do, if I wave my PhD around and talk smart (but not so smart that I sound threatening), then doors open, opportunities present themselves, my treatment improves, and jobs become available. In fact, this is, in many ways, how I landed my first professorship. I was twenty-three years old and had made all the right connections. Then I met a fairy godmother and received a dream teaching position.

At the time it was one of the most exciting moments of my life, and I was eager to prove that I was worthy of the job. My first order of business was to go shopping and buy an entire new wardrobe of clothes that seemed suitably "professor-y." You know, the pencil skirts and button-up blouses, the smart-looking jackets, and the heels that say, "I'm here to work." It wasn't Cinderella's blue dress, but it was a complete makeover nonetheless, and I felt like a new person as I stepped onto campus the first day of class. I looked every part the German professor. I had the clothes, the purse, the books. I even made myself a salad to eat for lunch that day (also a definite first).

Everything about class that day went perfectly. Afterward, I trekked back to the foreign language department, eager to mingle with other professors and discuss first-day experiences (but also to talk about how amazing my classes had gone). There were friendly smiles and a confluence of languages echoing down the hallway as I arrived. I found a few familiar faces in the copy room and joined their conversation on research and coursework, which ebbed and flowed from English to German and Spanish.

However, that all changed in a matter of minutes.

During our discussion, another new professor popped by to say hello. One of my colleagues kindly tried to introduce me, saying, "This is Michelle Reyes . . ." He said a few more things about me, like my research areas, which I was beginning to appreciate, but then suddenly he turned back to me and asked, "And remind me again what your ethnicity is. You're Indian, right?"

It's hard to even describe what a moment like this feels like. The minute he said those words, I felt like I had an out-of-body experience, like I was floating up near the ceiling and looking down at myself. I wasn't trying to draw attention to myself. I was simply doing what everyone else was doing, and yet I still stuck out. I didn't understand at first why he would single out my ethnicity when there was no need to do so, but the answer was simple: my efforts to conform could never hide my brown skin.

Even worse, I now felt ashamed. I thought to myself, "What have I done?" Standing there in my white button-up shirt and stiletto heels, I realized just how much I had given up to feel worthy in this predominantly white space. My cultural identity had been whitewashed. I dressed like my white peers. I talked like my white peers. I even changed my food to eat like they did. But even after all that, they weren't quite sure who I was.

You might be thinking, What's the big deal? Most professors dress up, right? Yes, it was an academic setting, but I had been overly sensitive about what clothes I should and shouldn't wear to work. There are formal Indian clothes that one *could* wear to work. But I never would have dreamed of wearing those on my first day. I had also been incredibly intentional about what words not to say. I never talked about my Indian identity during the hiring process or used colloquial phrases that would hint at my cultural background. I didn't bring any Indian food to eat that first day of school either.

Being an Indian American woman in the humanities brings unique challenges. Indians (and Asians in general) are typically not encouraged by their parents to study things like literature and art, and if you do meet an Asian American in the humanities, they probably have a story to tell about how their family didn't react well to the news that they weren't going to pursue medicine. So there I was, in a predominantly white department, trying to prove to my parents and my colleagues that I belonged.

However, hearing a colleague question my cultural identity was like a jolt to me. This happened during the early years of my cultural identity development, and I realized that I was not yet comfortable in my own skin. His words made me feel ashamed that I had given up, or maybe even lost, a part of my culture to be in this space. And I wasn't sure what to do with those feelings. Choosing to act white at that time was largely a survival strategy, but it also brought with it a lot of baggage.

Did acting professional mean acting white? Was it possible to be myself, to dress and act like an Indian American woman, and still be welcomed in a predominantly white workspace? Would Cinderella have been welcomed at the ball in her tattered clothes? At the time, I wasn't sure.

Code Switching Is Complicated

What I was doing at that time, without knowing it, has a formal name. It's called code switching, and honestly it's something we all do.[2] We all change ourselves in different scenarios, bending and reshaping our personalities to accommodate different situations, whether it's a date, a job interview, or hanging out with friends. For people of color, the practice of code switching constantly challenges our self-conception of identity and culture, making us question who we really are. It's the voice in your head that tells you, "You've got this—just act white." And in response we change our vocabulary, our inflection, and even our physical appearance to appear less like a minority, hiding aspects of ourselves to fit in.

I utilized code switching to present myself more like a white woman and less like myself, a bicultural Indian American woman. Code switching became a tool that allowed me to circumvent those uncomfortable situations, to put on a mask so as not to confuse people with my "otherness." As many of us are now learning, there is always a default or dominant culture. There is mainstream white American culture, and then there are Black and Brown subcultures. Many of us change our language and mannerisms depending on which culture we want to be accepted in.

Some of you may have never heard the term *code switching* before. Others reading this have been doing it every day of your life. Many of us have learned how to perform based on who is in the room. We know how to exercise high honor and respect when visiting aunts and uncles, while also making our names and stories sound more "American" to fit with the general population. We can barbecue like our neighbors on the weekends and eat homemade ethnic food during the week. We can act one way in the barber shop and another at work. We can even talk about Jesus, theology, and the Bible one way when visiting an all-white church and then change our tone and lingo when fellowshipping with Black and Brown Christians. We can be who we need to be so that we can become who we want to be.

I also recognize that code switching can be a point of pride for many people of color. If you feel that way, you don't need to be ashamed of your ability to do this. There's a difference between a minority being forced to alter their language to fit the status quo and a person who chooses to switch between different forms of expression of their own volition. Being bilingual or even trilingual can often empower individuals to craft unique and creative representations through language. When we have control over our own language, we can wield it to invent new words, mixings, and alternatives as forms of familial codes, as subversion, and even as resistance.[3] These kinds of mixings and fusions of language can reflect our complex identities in ways that make us feel special, and that's something to celebrate.

In short, it's a blessing and a curse as a person of color to code switch. Part of what it means to live in a multicultural society like ours is, to some degree, learning how to change and transform to fit into different contexts. But I also want to consider the complexity of code switching for historically disempowered people, who have been forced to do this their whole lives just to survive. The last thing I want people of color to hear is that the Scriptures' call to "become all things to all people" is merely a ploy for them to remain silent and lose their unique cultural heritage. We need to acknowledge there are power dynamics at work here as well as a long history of control by those in the dominant culture. We need to admit this and then seek to understand what cultural accommodation should look like, biblically speaking, for both majority and minority alike.

Biblical Servanthood Is Not What You Think

In discussions on freedom and rights it is all too common to find misinterpretations of the Bible, especially as they relate to the topic of slavery. Passages on slavery have been horribly misappropriated, abused, and weaponized by white Christians to oppress people of color, both in our country and around the world. We should use the word *slavery* sparingly and with caution.

So I'm cautiously approaching 1 Corinthians 9:19, where Paul says, "Though I am free and belong to no one, I have made myself a slave to everyone, to win as many as possible." This verse is the linchpin to Paul's discussion in verses 19–23 as he talks about Christians becoming all things to all people. But let me be very clear up front about what this passage does not mean and will never mean: Paul is not telling disadvantaged peoples that they should enslave themselves to the ruling elite. This verse is not telling Black and Brown people to accommodate to white people by hiding who they are. Paul does not use this verse to justify the silencing and erasure of historically disempowered peoples either. Before any discussion about 1 Corinthians 9:19, we need to be clear about what Paul is *not* saying. With that in mind, let's break the verse down, piece by piece, and see if we can understand what he *is* saying.

First, notice the word *free*. Paul begins 1 Corinthians 9:19 with a dramatic emphasis on his freedom, and that's important. Paul is free. He is free from people and their ideas. In fact, when Paul says he is free from people, he likely had a few different meanings in mind. Paul was free from the ultra-conservative Jews who demanded that he disentangle himself from Gentiles. He was free from the pressure to follow the mold of traveling "evangelists" who sought legitimacy based on their rhetoric and the revenue received from their audiences. Paul is also free from following what certain dogmatic elitists are telling him he must do.[4] Paul's discussion of freedom in 1 Corinthians 9:19 is similar to 1 Corinthians 7:17–24 where he exhorts the Corinthians not to become "slaves of human beings." The point in both of these passages is that he will never be enslaved to the *ideas* of other people.

Conformity was as much of an issue in the first century as it is today. The intellectual elite in Corinth had certain ideas about how everyone should behave. Not only did they set the standard for normative behavior and practices, they also expected people to cater to their personal expressions. For example, while Paul was in Corinth, the elites wanted him to speak differently. They felt that his vocabulary lacked a certain eloquence, but as we see in 1 Corinthians 1–4 Paul repeatedly rejects their demands.[5] In fact, he is quick to point out that their request stems from their upper-class ideology with its overemphasis on Greco-Roman linguistics. These leaders want Paul to speak like they do, thereby reflecting *their* status and cultural identity, and Paul refuses to have any part of this. He will not appease the wealthy and the powerful. That is his freedom and his right.

So when Paul says that he is "free and belong[s] to no one," he is saying that, in Christ, he is free from the systems and institutions of this world. Our allegiance is to King Jesus, and we follow his command and guidance. No one else. God gives those who belong to him this right—a God-given right to exercise cultural freedom—and I believe this right has immediate application for us today. In like fashion, a person of color should never be enslaved by the codes of a white person. A Black man should never be forced to give up his rights to fit into a white space. A Brown woman has the right to be herself, and she should never have to feel like she has to hide her identity or change her speech just so that her ideas will be heard. Paul is making it very clear that becoming all things to all people is never about disempowerment.

Paul makes one caveat though. There is one person we should serve: the Lord. And how do we serve the Lord? By sharing the good news of Jesus Christ. This is what Paul is referring to when he says, "I have made myself a slave to everyone, to win as many as possible." In other words, Paul is willing to give up certain freedoms or rights for the sake of winning people for Christ. If ever there was a time he would consider altering a part of his identity, behavior, or speech, it would be within the context of evangelism. Here Paul is being strategic, recognizing that when the gospel is at stake, connecting with people of other cultures may come at a personal cost. This is a cost he's willing to bear, so long as it is part of his service to God and not because he has been forced to cater to the whims or preferences of specific individuals.[6]

This is the crux of Paul's argument. If he sacrifices some

of his rights, it's not to experience disempowerment but for another purpose. He temporarily gives up certain freedoms in order to "win" people. The word *win* here is unique. In fact, 1 Corinthians 9:19 is the only place where Paul uses the verb *win* in this way. The only other occurrence of the word in his writings is in Philippians 3:8 where he writes of gaining Christ. It's a word used primarily in the context of conversion. Someone is won for Christ from darkness or from the world. The Greek word for "win" means "to gain or acquire by investment,"[7] and this definition provides us a useful lens for understanding why Paul enslaves himself to achieve this kind of acquisition. This is not slavery by our modern understanding, in which a slave is not free to do as he wishes. Rather, Paul's choice to make himself a slave is deliberate, something he chooses by his own free will as an investment toward the salvation of others. In other words, Paul gives up his rights for salvific purposes only, and this nuance, as well as discernment, is needed to understand what Paul means by being free and a slave. In other words, we can adapt our cultural expressions, our rights, and our freedoms for evangelistic purposes.

So what do these two terms, *free* and *slave*, mean as we think about engaging in cross-cultural relationships today? Let's start with the first term, *free*. Each one of you is free. You are free in Christ. You were created purposefully as a cultural being, and part of reflecting the glory and image of God is to express your cultural values in word, action, and dress. This is the freedom that God gives us. We are free to be all that we were made to be, and I pray you find this truth both empowering and liberating.

We were not created to be enslaved to other people—physically, culturally, or ideologically. We were not created to change our workplace appearance merely to conform to a particular standard. We were not created to hide our foods or our mother tongue simply because other people tell us these things make them uncomfortable. We were not created to change our bodies, our beauty standards, or our communal values simply because they are not valued in majority US society. Embrace the way God has created you as a cultural being, and embrace it proudly.

It also means that the question we should be asking ourselves is not, "What do I need to change about myself to fit in?" but rather, "*When* can I adapt my words, behavior, or dress for the sake of the gospel?"

A Word to My Sisters and Brothers of Color

The conversation on giving up one's rights is never about seeking relationships that produce perpetual hurt. You are not required to take on the burden of changing the hearts and minds of individual racists when they are abusive toward you. If there is any kind of verbal, physical, or emotional abuse, then you shouldn't be in those relationships.

That being said, as people of color, I want us to reconsider our engagement with a whole spectrum of people. Our engagement with both white people and fellow people of color will look different because each group has a different history with distinct power dynamics at work.

About White People

I don't know if you've ever heard someone say this before, but it's true: you can and should be yourself in white spaces. If you've spent your whole life code switching, learning to be yourself will take practice. It's going to be hard at first. You will need to be bold and, in the words of Kathy Khang, "raise your voice," and you'll need to expect some confusion and pushback as well.[8] It's okay to say, "Well, actually, that's not quite right," and proudly share the real facts about your heritage, your identity, and the right way to pronounce your name. You don't have to hide who you are.

When you, as a minority, are engaging with white people, your aim should be to avoid code switching. To use the words of W. E. B. Du Bois, we need to shed our double consciousness,[9] while still learning how to stretch ourselves to connect with well-meaning albeit ignorant white people—many of the white people you have as friends in your workplace, in your neighborhood, and in your church. Their hearts may be in the right place, but they are likely unaware of the impact of their words and actions. Many of them have no idea that the policies they have in place, the way they direct a meeting, or how they converse with you is hurtful and wrong. Don't give up on these people. The model of Christ instructs us not to burn bridges.

How have historically disempowered people of color embraced Paul's challenge to become "a slave to everyone" (1 Cor. 9:19)? *Love.* Every time a white person unwittingly wields the ideology or the vernacular of white supremacy, we have the right to be angry. We have the right to challenge these ideas and work toward dismantling unjust systems. But because we serve Christ, we must do these things by speaking truth *in love*. We respond to painful encounters with a demand for justice in the form of holistic restoration and a pursuit of peace.[10] Rev. Dr. Martin Luther King Jr. once said, "One day, we must come to see that peace is not merely a distant goal we seek, but that it is a means by which we arrive at that goal. We must pursue peaceful ends through peaceful means."[11] This is not about staying silent. It's about challenging the status quo while also having peace and unity as the goal.

Love is patient and kind. It is not self-seeking. Love chooses to endure. When we choose love, we also ask God for the strength and the courage to lean in when a white person ignorantly voices racial biases. Why? Because you know the other person needs to hear the gospel. Love means choosing to work with someone who might even be hostile to cultures outside their own, but you do so because your goal is to plant gospel seeds. Love means stepping into a predominantly white space, if (and only if) the Lord calls you to it, and figuring out how to lay the foundation for lasting connections between white people and people of color. You can stretch yourself to be humble, kind, and perseverant without hiding or being ashamed of your cultural identity. You are free in Christ, and nobody can take that freedom away from you.

About Fellow Minorities

Just because minorities have historically been without power, it doesn't mean we are immune to privilege. We also must come to grips with the fact that every community of color, both Black and Brown, has people with privileges that others within that community don't have. Yes, we share in common the reality that every community of color suffers oppression because of the color of our skin. Yet we also must recognize that not every single person within the community is treated the same.

We must acknowledge, as author Ijeoma Oluo argues, that "some of our own are more negatively impacted by things like white supremacy and systems of oppression than we are—those who, unlike us, can't cushion some of the blows of racism with at least some of the indicators of success valued by white people that we ourselves have been able to secure."[12] That, at its core, is what privilege means. It's advantages you have that others do not, and these advantages allow you to experience injustice in our country to a lesser degree. This is one reason we still need to talk about interminority relationships as we discuss code switching. Ethnocentrism and tribalism exist, and we are equally capable of creating hierarchies among fellow people of color.

I see this reflected in my own life. Yes, I've had to work very hard for what I've accomplished, but even my story of struggle within higher education speaks to my privilege. I have a college degree, a middle-class job, and connections to white communities. I have eclectic tastes in music and food. I don't live under the poverty line (not anymore), and most of my friends of color are people who talk, think, and act like me. But it would be wrong of me to look down on fellow people of color who don't have similar degrees or who aren't as critically minded as I am. I used to be quite proud and think less of people of color who didn't have aspirations to climb the social ladder or conform to white standards. Then I began to recognize my privilege and saw that not every person of color has had the same opportunities and points of access that I've had. The deck hasn't been stacked against all of us equally.

Colorism is one example of how this disparity exists among minorities. This is a by-product of racism that creates hierarchies *within* minority races based on skin tones. If you are a person of color with fairer skin, you may have benefited from unfair privileges because of your lighter skin tone, receiving better grades, job offers, or financial success over other minorities who were wrongly deemed more threatening or less trustworthy because of their darker complexion. Our lack of disadvantage in this area may even be a blinder preventing us from fully understanding the depth of the struggle. We need to call out colorism and any other disadvantage created by white supremacy, no matter what it might cost us. We don't need to operate under the mentality of scarcity. There are enough resources and opportunities for every person of color. We need to be willing to have the hard conversations, assert our right to be heard and seen just as we are, and humble ourselves so we can love all the different and unique people of color around us. How can we serve each other? What freedoms or privileges might we need to reconsider in order to fully love and care for fellow members of subdominant cultures?

As people of color, we can be both privileged in some areas and underprivileged in others.[13] Both can be true at once and can impact our life at the same time. The challenge of Paul in 1 Corinthians 9:19 is for us to consider where we benefit most, where we hold power over fellow minorities, and then to seek to dismantle that privilege in pursuit of true equality for all people of color. Learning how to serve each other as people of color is part of our Christian witness. It's how we point each other to Jesus.

Fellow brothers and sisters of color, let's lean into who God has made us to be. Bring that homemade lunch to school. Proudly wear those ethnic clothes. Don't hide your accent or the natural waves of your hair or the way you actually think about something. Do all of these things while also having a spiritual radar, a sensitivity to know when you should adapt yourself to those around you for the sake of the gospel. We should never have to erase our God-given cultural identity. But we can learn to lovingly and humbly care for both white people and fellow people of color for the sake of following Jesus.

Remember that you are free. God himself declares this to be true. Christ is the only Lord we serve, and he has empowered us with true freedom to adapt ourselves to the physical and spiritual livelihoods of the people around us.

Avoid Cultural Appropriation

I'll never forget the first time I walked into a custom kitchen, the kind you see on HGTV with vintage runners, English-style cabinetry, and framed art. Just imagine that in shades of olive and gray, and that's where I found myself. My husband and I were at the home of new acquaintances for dinner, and the minute we walked into their kitchen, my jaw dropped almost instinctively. It was undoubtedly the biggest kitchen I had ever seen with granite counters surrounding me on every side. All I could think about was how this would be *the* perfect space for my whole family to cook and eat together (because gatherings around food is where my mind naturally trails). Seriously, my whole family could fit around the island counter alone.

The most remarkable section of this kitchen was an entire wall that had been devoted to an eight-piece stove. The whole thing looked like a page from the *Magnolia Journal* with its farmhouse flair. The stove was framed on each side with large glass cabinets stocked with spices in every color you can imagine.

And that's when I saw it.

Right in the center of this menagerie of spices was a bright yellow bottle labeled "curry." I turned to our hosts in surprise and asked, "Y'all cook Indian food?" They looked nothing but confused by my comment. So I pointed back at the bottle and said, "You have a curry jar in your cabinet."

"Oh that?" the woman replied with a laugh. "I bought that because the color makes the whole spice cabinet pop. Isn't it pretty?"

"Huh," I thought to myself. The idea of a decorative spice, at that time, was foreign to me. I didn't even fully understand what that meant.

Food is deeply personal for me. It's closely linked to my identity as an Indian American woman. It doesn't matter that I have plain wooden cabinets that you can't see through. I know the power of the spices they hold and the stories they weave in my own cultural journey. So many second-generation immigrants like myself have experienced loss after loss in our culture—much of my clothing is now Western, my language is Western—and food is one of the last cultural domains that I have. Through food, I express Indian values like hospitality and communal gatherings. It's also how I feel most connected with my ancestors. The dishes I learned to cook with my mother are the same that her mother passed on to her. When I cook kadhi and khichdi, I'm doing more than simply making dinner. I'm reaching into my past, connecting with my grandmother in a deeply personal way, and continuing our cultural legacy.

But none of my story mattered at that moment. This non-Indian kitchen had a bottle of curry completely devoid of my culture's heritage and purpose, and I was struggling to make sense of that.

"You mean you've never cooked with it before?" I asked, still in shock. The woman laughed again and replied, "Oh goodness, no. I have no idea what I'd do with that. Isn't curry a strong flavor? I would *not* want my kitchen smelling like that."

Those words stung, and my confusion was turning to pain.

How many times had I felt the shame of eating alone because nobody wanted to sit next to the girl with the smelly homemade lunch? I have memories of the kids at school dramatically holding their noses, coughing loudly, or pointing and laughing, all to let me know their disdain for the smells of my Indian food. For a time during my adolescence, I didn't even want to eat Indian food. There was so much shame and pain and insecurity that had come from those childhood experiences. There were years that I found myself eating only typical American foods so I could fit in, be liked, and have friends, even though I secretly longed for nothing more than a hot plate of chana masala, pooris, and a cup of mango lassi on the side.

Of course, our hosts didn't know this. That little yellow spice had no personal meaning for them. Without missing a beat they then casually asked, "Do you guys cook with curry?"

Internally I was shouting, "What are these people saying?! Do they not know the name of a single Indian dish?

Do they think there is a type of Indian food *called* curry?" I didn't know where to begin. But they had asked me a question, and I needed to say something, so the words began stumbling out.

"Well," I replied, "the thing is . . . curry is simply a reference to different spice combinations, like cumin, coriander, turmeric, and garam masala. Every Indian dish has a different combination of spices, so in a sense every Indian dish has curry in it."

"Oh!" both our hosts exclaimed. "We didn't know that."

"Yeah," I continued. "For example, my mom's family is from the state of Gujarat in northwest India. We eat things like rotli, kadhi or dal, rice, and shaak. The spice combinations we use are different from other states in India. In Gujarati dal, we use hing, black mustard seeds, and even a pinch of sugar. No one else makes dal that way. Talking about Indian food is like comparing cuisines from the Midwest and the South here in the United States. They're just all very different from each other."

I thought this would spark some interest for my hosts. Instead, it was followed by the most bizarre part of our conversation thus far. The woman calmly replied with a placid smile, "That's nice. . . . So, is anyone hungry?" And with that we weirdly segued to dinner, and our discussion moved elsewhere.

That bottle of curry powder haunted me during our meal together. A symbol of my culture had been relegated to a useless place in someone else's home. This couple was treating curry as an accessory, devoid of its context and original use, and this is, by definition, the very essence of cultural appropriation. I know my hosts didn't have malicious intent, but at the same time Americans have become so used to spice racks and fusion cuisines that we've lost our sensitivity to the appropriation of other cultures' food. The co-opting of spices has a long history that precedes our modern debates on appropriation, like who should be allowed to wear what costume for Halloween or the mimicking of accents. Whole civilizations have been shaped by the desire for spice. Writer Roxana Hadadi explains, "The spice trade helped build the Silk Road and expand the palates of ancient empires, who in turn traded for, and sometimes just stole, resources from other areas of the world, including China, India, Persia, and Sri Lanka. Later, through colonization and subjugation of huge swaths of the world, those spices became sought after by other cultures too. Think of the English, the Portuguese, the French, the Dutch."[1] This is a history that is as old as time. However, because many of us don't understand that the "foreign" spices in our cabinets were acquired by spilled blood, we find ourselves now in a situation where the average Westerner doesn't acknowledge the people and cultures he or she is borrowing from. Many people even laugh at or insult traditional food, all while having the privilege of using any spice they please without trying to pay due respect to the culture it came from. This is why I was upset that day in our new friends' home. Deep and complicated narratives are at work. And, if this couple didn't understand the beauty of this bottle of curry, I feared that they wouldn't understand or appreciate me, an actual Indian, sitting in front of them.

This Is Not about Cultural Policing

Perhaps you know where I'm coming from. Or perhaps you feel like I'm making too big a deal about who eats what. One time I had a friend tell me, "We live in a multicultural society, right? Fusions are going to happen. That's, after all, how we have things like Tex-Mex and rap music."[2] More than that, in the twenty-first century, many feel that cultural appropriation— like globalization—isn't just inevitable; it's potentially positive. Isn't it a good thing to eat foods from all different cultures and attend things like ethnic festivals? Why should you be penalized for trying to appreciate other cultures?

If this is how you feel, to an extent, I understand where you're coming from. Particularly for people of European descent, there's fear around conversations about cultural appropriation, because the alternative sounds like just staying in your own cultural lane and eating nothing but Gruyere cheese, fish and chips, or Swedish meatballs. You don't want to have your life policed by people who seem like they're jealously tracking down who owns what and instantly jumping on transgressors.[3]

But that is not my intent.

Our aim should not be to impose cultural regulations on who gets to do what. Instead, we should focus on how to live in a way that is respectful of other people's cultures—their food, art, music, and traditions—and understand them in their context. If I become upset at people buying bottles of curry as aesthetic ornaments, it's not because I'm trying to control who is allowed to buy and use curry in their cooking.

Rather, I am objecting to the *manner* in which these things are done. Is it respectful? Does someone's use of a certain cultural item—a spice, a type of food, an article of clothing, a decoration, dance moves, a song, even language—enrich the lives of people in that cultural group or cheapen them? When we purchase, consume, or wear something from someone else's culture, will they feel honored or mocked, advantaged or disadvantaged?

In a fluid, multicultural society, cultural items will ebb and flow between peoples. For example, I now cook Mexican food alongside Indian dishes because I'm married to a second-generation Mexican immigrant, and his story has become a part of mine. He likes listening to Spanish music and dancing merengue, and I do too now. Expanding our cultural palates and expressions can be beautiful when a relationship lies at the core and when we take responsibility to do it in a way that respects and cherishes the people who grew up in that culture. When we celebrate Día de Muertos as a family, I'm careful to incorporate the decorations, foods, and traditions that my husband grew up with and to treat the day with care. Context, personal connections, and sensitivity are all present.

But we also have to recognize that our use of someone else's cultural items can also directly hurt or disadvantage them. We can't avoid the issue of unequal power dynamics because its access and exchange does not always exist on an equal playing field. If you are of European descent and the country of your ancestors was never colonized or enslaved, you will probably feel less threatened if someone wants to wear clogs or learn how to cook lefse. We don't all share equal histories of oppression and enslavement, and when other people partake of your food or engage in your traditions, it's possible that your culture is not being threatened by cultural erasure. That, however, is exactly the danger when dominant cultures create hybridized forms of subdominant cultural elements. Every time an ethnic food is "Americanized," a part of its origin, and with it the identity of a people group, has the potential to be lost. This is why so many minorities talk about cultural appropriation in terms of loss. Food, clothing, and the arts, for many of us, are some of the last strongholds of our cultural identity, and when other people begin to experiment with these things, part of who we are as an African American, Puerto Rican, Cuban, Filipino, Latino, Afro-Caribbean, Indian, Mexican, Colombian, or Cheyenne feels threatened. It is important to see this so you understand why subdominant peoples speak out so strongly at times when they feel elements of their culture have been misappropriated.

This is also why we need a definition of cultural appropriation that moves beyond simple concepts of cultural sharing. Cultural appropriation happens when elements are taken from a subdominant culture, and not only is nothing offered in return, but the expectation is that the people should be grateful for the promotion. This can include "trying on" another ethnic identity by wearing costumes while the people of that culture who live within their skin, hair, and culture struggle for acceptance. Consider, for example, the ongoing debate as to whether white people should wear ethnic costumes.[4] Many people nonchalantly don an outfit or headdress (or paint their face a different color), all while completely ignoring the larger historical context, including the pain and suffering that are often tied to these identities. For example, I was shamed as a child for wearing traditional Indian clothes in public. Saris, bangles, and braided hair signaled my otherness, and yet when white women wear Indian clothes, either for fun at a party, for belly dancing, or on a mission trip to India, they are complimented as beautiful. This is a disparity. People are taking a piece of my culture and wearing it as a costume, which has the potential of co-opting my story and undermining my worth and value, as well as my experiences of pain.

Let me put it this way: cultural appropriation is the act of superimposing one's own understandings of another culture over the actual culture and treating it as a cheap accessory.[5] This is largely a problem for those who are in the dominant or majority culture, wherever that is across the globe. Here in the United States, the majority culture has grown accustomed to stepping in and out of other cultural spaces and appropriating bits and pieces as needed. Now that there has been pushback and criticism, many people in the dominant culture are upset—even though there have been centuries with zero accountability. The real problem is the failure to recognize complicity in mining other people's cultures, without regard for what the cultural artifact might mean to those who created it or who benefits from the appropriation.[6] Only those who enjoy the benefits of privilege fail to see the problem—of taking and repurposing things without permission and without care for how this might impact real people.

Permissible versus Beneficial

Disagreements about participation in another culture's food and practices, however, are nothing new. In the first century AD, elitist Christians claimed to have superior knowledge of the culture at large. These were smart, educated people, and they had no shame demanding the right to eat and drink whatever they wanted. Sound familiar?

The apostle Paul spends a good deal of 1 Corinthians rebuking these Christians for their attitudes and actions. In fact, when Paul writes that he seeks to be all things to all people in 1 Corinthians 9:19–23, it's part of a larger commentary on culture, and food in particular, that he constructs from 1 Corinthians 8 through 11:1. Some of the Christians he addresses want to eat foods made by Gentiles—not just any food but dishes dedicated to pagan gods. Paul's main concern is their arrogance and lack of concern for other people. These Christians argue that since they *know* food sacrificed to idols is not real, there is no problem in eating it. However, Paul points out that their flippant approach to a religious food artifact is causing people to stumble into sin, and he tells them to stop.

Paul's rebuke is based on a simple principle: the Christian life is not about what you can do—your rights and privileges—but what you're willing to give up to lovingly serve others. In fact, he tells them twice in 1 Corinthians, "'I have the right to do anything,' you say—but not everything is beneficial. 'I have the right to do anything'—but not everything is constructive. No one should seek their own good, but the good of others" (6:12; 10:23–24). In other words, when addressing topics like food and other cultural activities, the principles of building up and benefiting the community are of utmost priority.[7]

Some of us are likely guilty of overemphasizing cultural experiences. We enjoy eating at ethnic restaurants; many of us take gap years after college and travel overseas; some of us have explicitly non-Western décor in our homes and apartments. These can all be good things when we're seeking to learn about and honor other people's cultures and put ourselves in the position of a student. My suspicion, however, is that we can often be drawn to other people's cultures and foods simply because they are beautiful, exciting, and different and feel eye-opening. When this happens, our priority becomes more about how much fun we can have, how "pretty" we've decorated our space, or how the experience is supposed to change us as a person, which is an incredibly individualistic approach to culture. We lose the focus on context and the importance of building relationships, and that's a problem. This is why we need to reconsider our actions and practices. Just because we *can* celebrate any cultural holiday, visit any country around the world, or cook or buy any kind of food doesn't mean we *should*; at the very least, we may need to consider if there is a better approach.[8]

The reality in the first century was that some Christians were asserting their right to eat whatever they wanted, but they were overlooking the context of the food and its original meaning (i.e., that it had been sacrificed to idols). Their actions confused people and even turned them away from the faith.

This is the issue that Paul seeks to address in 1 Corinthians, and it remains relevant today. Our enjoyment of food or other elements of a culture can sometimes be entirely divorced from any connection with the people of that culture, and this is a reality that creates genuine hurt and misunderstanding with damaging effects on people and communities of color. For example, people say they love chips and queso or breakfast tacos, but they don't have any interest in engaging with real-life Mexicans. People buy toy tepees for their kids without any thought or care of how this looks and feels to local Native American communities. I've even seen white people organize their own Holi party, an Indian holiday that celebrates the coming of spring, with pictures on social media of them throwing paint at each other, as is customary on that day. But do any of them have a single Indian friend? Were Indians even invited to their party, let alone asked to organize it? Not so much. The point is that real-life relationships must drive our impulse and desire to connect across cultures. We need to take conscious steps to engage communities of people and reconsider the consequences of superficial engagement with another person's culture.

To be clear, I'm not saying that if you are not Mexican, you can't eat at a taqueria (or if you're a white chef, you can't make a flauta). I'm not saying that if you're not Indian, you can't eat chicken tikka masala. But I'm asking you to take a step further. Consider *why* you participate in or engage with cultural activities or food outside your own culture. As Christians, our focus should be whether the foods we eat and drink, as well as the clothes we wear, the music we listen to and the decorations in our homes, build up the community they represent. There's no law that says you can't attend a Chinese New Year festival or wear a cable-knit cardigan with a tribal design. But ask yourself: Does my participation in or use of these things benefit that people group?

This brings me back to our discussion on accommodation and appropriation. The lesson that we learn from Paul in 1 Corinthians 8:1–11:1 is that our participation in food and other cultural activities should *only* be done in context and for the purpose of gaining greater access to people's lives and, even more importantly, for their good. Being "woke" (i.e., well informed on issues of culture and race) is not an authentic mark of a true Christian. Instead, as Paul makes clear in the pivotal thirteenth chapter of 1 Corinthians, love must be our defining marker. And to love someone means that you seek their advantage. In 1 Corinthians, we see that the Greek word for "benefit" implies "bringing together," but its meaning in the discussion of 6:12 and 10:23–24 means to build up. Paul's frequent use of this word throughout his letter in deliberate rhetoric is an appeal to advantage. When we love someone, we proactively speak and act in ways that are for their advantage.[9] That is true love. Paul says that "knowledge puffs up while love builds up" (1 Cor. 8:1). In other words, make sure that your words and actions are for the loving benefit of your neighbors.

This is why we must engage with other cultures on more than an aesthetic level. Consider what America might be like if people loved Mexicans as much as they loved tacos. How would our society be different if people loved the Black community as much as they loved their music (e.g., hip-hop, R&B, blues, etc.)? When we are engaging with real people across a cultural spectrum, our cultural knowledge will naturally increase. As we listen to real people, we learn what brings them both joy and pain. We learn what is sacred to them, whether values or objects, and why we should not borrow these for our own purposes and agendas. If someone tells you they feel their culture is being appropriated, don't get mad. Listen, seek to understand, and be willing to take a different step forward.

We shouldn't pick and choose between people and their cultural artifacts. If we want to truly enjoy another culture—their lifestyle, narratives, clothing, country, music, and food—we first need to bond with someone of that culture. We will need to eat with them, learn to have fun with them, and seek to better understand what affects them, what bothers them, and what they feel is unfair. Our focus is on people and what matters to them, not utilizing objects for our benefit or enjoyment.

Let's Start Here

This might sound overwhelming. There are so many people groups and individualized cultures, and it will take time to deconstruct the layers of cultural appropriation in each of our lives. You won't be able to do this overnight. But we have to start somewhere, taking small steps to grow in relationships with others. Here are three tangible practices you can begin implementing today.

Reconsider What It Means to Be Authentic

I distinctly remember the year I stopped drinking Starbucks coffee. I had become tired of commodified products from the corporate world and was longing for something more natural and, of course, personalized to my taste. I've reached that point in my life where I want the foods I eat and the clothes I wear to have a measurable effect on the health of my body and the quality of my life. I'm tired of false promises and fake products, preferring something real and authentic instead, so that I can define myself in relation to a set of ethics and aesthetics, not brands. The worst thing I could be, in my opinion, is another "mindless consumer," and I know I'm not alone in feeling this way.

There is much that I love about responsible, local shopping, but for many of us, our fetish for authenticity has a dark side as well. Seeking what is real and authentic can lead to mining other cultures. Consider the popularity of chai tea lattes, for example. This is a drink consumed daily by millions of Indians across the world. It's ethnically different, yet can also be developed locally and organically. You can buy artisanal chai concentrate almost anywhere, from your local supermarket to Costco, and every local café has its own unique blend (although none of these Americanized forms of chai taste anything like the tea you'd drink in my home). There is also the problem of repeating ourselves when we call it "chai." *Chai* in Hindi means "tea," so when people say "chai tea," they're essentially saying "tea tea." The real concern with the crafting and consuming of chai tea lattes in the United States is that it is an example of *Columbusing*.

This term refers to a situation where something a white person has "discovered" as exotic and unique is utterly ordinary and commonplace for an entire people group (think also of when a white woman claimed that she had invented the hair bonnet, an accessory used by Black women for centuries). To put it simply: a non-Indian coffee shop can't claim to have a new or original blend of chai. It doesn't matter if you make your own caramelized sugar as a topping and you took twelve hours to marinate it. You cannot claim authenticity—having something real and truly representative—for a cultural object you recently discovered. Instead of highlighting your discovery or your unique blend or adaptation of the original, put the focus on the culture whose products you enjoy. Highlight the people who originally created it and see yourself as a part of *their* story. This holds true for everything from avocado toast and barbecue to anything with the word *craft* attached to it.

We need to be more cautious and respectful when we utilize elements of other people's cultures in our pursuit of what is real and authentic. Beware of cultural plagiarism. Do not take the defining elements of a person's culture—their stories, objects, and artifacts—and make them your own without giving proper citation. These ethnic treasures—the collective traditions and practices of the world's people groups—are not *our* undiscovered treasure trove, full of resources to be mined and exploited.

Choose Your Words Wisely

I once had a Jewish friend tell me she was tired of hearing Christians use words like *goy* and *non-goy* (Hebrew words for

Gentile and non-Gentile). She felt frustrated that instead of getting to know her as a Jewish woman it seemed like people were trying to impress her with the few Hebrew words they knew. The use of isolated terminology is another example of cultural appropriation within a majority culture, and it suffers from a problem similar to the use of food or clothing from another culture. Many of things we do or say in isolation have too much historical and linguistic baggage to be used so casually.

Hear me on this: I'm not trying to police your every word. I recognize that English, like every language, has a history of mixing and adopting new words. My point here is not about whether you're allowed to say words like *spiel*, *macho*, or *faux pas* but whether you should consider the motive behind your use of such words. Our motivations can often be misguided, especially when we utilize borrowed phrases and behaviors to appear smart or as surface-level proof that we are culturally sensitive. Using words from another language or culture flippantly or out of their original context, however, can be offensive. Isolated words have the capacity of becoming weaponized mechanisms that hurt cultural communities, diminish their distinctions, and create pale, watered-down rehashes instead. I have in mind the white person visiting an Indian restaurant who greets an Indian by saying, "Namaste," with awkward hands and bows. Or the person who tries to use slang that he or she heard in a movie with a person from a different culture. Your intention may be to use these isolated phrases as a cultural tool to connect with someone, but in reality these attempts are often perceived at best as impersonal, and at worst as offensive—a modern-day form of colonialism. In most cases, I'd wager you are doing more harm than good.

A good litmus test for knowing when to use certain terms is to consider whether you would use that word with everyone you know or just with isolated individuals. If you call all your white friends by their first name but refer to your lone Latino friend as something else (like "homey" or "dawg"), there is a problematic discrepancy. Trust me, that person of color does not feel grateful you have made them hypervisible and treated them differently. Give people of other cultures the same respectful treatment that you give your friends from your own ethnic heritage, and instead of appropriating someone else's cultural expressions, consider how you can utilize your own cultural codes to express yourself.

Support *Real* Locals

It should be our goal to support local ethnic vendors, entrepreneurs, and restaurants. Plain and simple, eating tacos at a gentrified restaurant will in no way benefit your local Latino community. Gentrification is one of the largest and most physical manifestations of cultural appropriation, and it is important to understand how the gentrification of a neighborhood hurts the local culture.

Gentrification occurs when original residents of a community, usually the poor and people of color, are displaced by wealthier white people.[10] When this happens, neighborhoods become flooded with new shops and restaurants that often *claim* to reflect the original community and its inhabitants. In East Austin, for example, a white-owned restaurant with the word *bodega* in its name moved into a neighborhood that is historically home to Spanish-speaking, working-class citizens. But for a restaurant run by white people, using the name *bodega* is problematic. While *bodega* has come to mean "corner store" thanks to Nuyorican (New York Puerto Rican) immigrants, this usage is not common throughout much of Latin America, and some take it as evidence of white people lumping together everyone from Spanish-speaking countries. But the greater concern is that the restaurant uses repurposed Latin imagery and language to sell plates priced around twenty dollars apiece, a price few of the historic locals can afford.

The unsavory truth of gentrification is that everything comes down to money. Our perceptions of various vendors and stores have financial implications, and these directly affect stores' and restaurants' bottom lines. Buying a Mexican rebozo shawl at an American chain store will cost three times more than purchasing it at a local Mexican bakery or shop. Ethnically inspired items like embroidered purses, man-bags, decorative mugs, and jewelry are for sale at higher retail cost in big name stores. And not only are these stores making money off another culture, they are taking money away from local, ethnic stores. In these cases, white people who own these stores can claim that they've made traditional ethnic clothes "sturdier" or certain foods "cleaner" and "healthier," but essentially they have now made these products more palatable and accessible to other white people. They're catalyzing a process that causes authentic individual cultures to be whitewashed with the latest trends, and this process is usually embedded with a measure of condescension toward the culture and its people too. Saying you've made something from another culture "better" is both disrespectful and insulting.

Don't believe the lie that gentrification makes neighborhoods better. It is simply, as Michelle Warren writes, the idea that a community of color "has the potential to be desirable to those who are fast enough, smart enough, and well-positioned enough to take it without feeling badly."[11] It is part of the economic machine of supply and demand, and the only way to combat these kinds of forces is to invest your time, money, and resources into helping local ethnic shops and restaurants survive. Eating and shopping at authentic locales may mean going out of your way, driving a longer distance, or planning ahead. But we should consider making these small sacrifices because, as Christians, supporting local cultures is part of how we share values, visions, and economics across cultures in loving and respectful ways

Again, to put it simply: if you take from another culture without awareness of or respect for the people of that culture, you open yourself up to accusations of cultural appropriation. If, instead, you engage with the culture, mingle with people from that culture, and listen to their stories with the goal of long-term relationships, you may still make mistakes along the way, but chances are you are on the right track.

Chapter 6

Don't Expect People to Come to You

I was pulling into the parking lot of our local grocery store when I saw two women walking toward me. I was pretty sure I knew one of them, but the last time I had seen her had been months ago. She wasn't someone I knew well—a friend of a friend—the kind of person that when someone asks, "How do you know each other?" there's an awkward pause as you begin asking yourself the same question. I knew she lived in the area, but I was wracking my brain to remember where I had last seen her and how we were connected.

From the way she greeted me, however, you'd have thought we were besties. There were big smiles and hugs, and an "Oh my goodness! It is *so* good to see you!" And that's when things got a little weird. She turned to the other woman with her and said, "This is my *friend*, Michelle."

Now, don't get me wrong. I was happy to see her, albeit still a bit confused. And it was nice to be called a friend. But

I had a sense that she was treating me a little "friendlier" than our acquaintance warranted. As an Indian American woman, I wouldn't consider us super close if you've never invited me over to your home or if we've never eaten together or hung out one-on-one. We'd mostly just bumped into each other occasionally at local events. I was pretty sure I'd only ever seen her or run into her on her own turf, like at this grocery store. We didn't have much in common.

Speaking of which, whenever I go to this particular local grocery store, I'm keenly aware of the fact that I've entered the lone white neighborhood in East Austin. I shop here because it is the only grocery store within a five-mile radius of my home. That's an entirely different problem. In our predominantly low-income, minority community populated with convenience stores, it is a continual struggle to find healthy quality food. So if I want anything better than processed, canned foods, I need to shop at this grocery store, even though it is like entering a different world of white culture filled with mopeds, craft beer, and guitars.

On the flip side, white people rarely visit my part of town, and fewer still want to live in my neighborhood. We've all heard the reasons why: our communities are not safe and coming here means leaving behind the "good, law-abiding" people, the excellent schools, and the strong property values. You don't come to live in my neighborhood if you're interested in things like green belts and community pools. You certainly don't consider bringing your kids to play at our playgrounds or eat at one of our local barbecue shops. It's too "dangerous." The crime rates are "too high." Someone might even try to sell you drugs or steal your car.

I love my neighborhood. It's full of rich culture and loving neighbors. But outsiders don't see that. People look at the Black and Brown people living there and formulate their own perceptions of our neighborhood, assuming it is riddled with crime. Their prejudice feels like an insurmountable hurdle at times.

All of this is background to my run-in with this "friend" at the grocery store that day. I'm probably the lone brown-skinned Indian American woman who shops there, and it is in this place that I run into all my white friends. And here is why the over-friendliness bothers me: I often get the feeling that white people want to prove to me how nice they are *because* I'm a person of color. They don't go out of their way to connect with me. They won't drive to my neighborhood or visit my home. But if I happen to cross paths with them in their all-white community, they want to make sure I see them. I'm sure some people do this to make me feel more at ease. They assume I must feel shy or nervous or intimidated (perhaps because I'm Brown), and a protective instinct kicks in. Sometimes it may be to give themselves a pat on the back so that they can check "Be nice to a person of color today" off their to-do list. Whatever the reason, it's never fun or enjoyable. I end up feeling like I'm on display, and instead of people talking to me, they start talking about me.

Many of my white friends have never visited my home. I have to drag my kids into our car and drive to their home on the other side of town if we have a playdate or a coffee hangout. For some reason, whenever I suggest coming over to our house or going to one of our local playgrounds, "the drive is too far," or they're "just too busy this week." But they're never too busy for me to come to see them. It doesn't add up, and it has made me wonder why people want to visit with me in the first place.

That's what made this interaction so uncomfortable. My "friend" eagerly turned to the other woman with her and introduced me this way: "So, Michelle is Indian, and her husband is Mexican, and we just love them." I awkwardly smiled, nodding a "yeah" in reply. Because I couldn't think of anything nice to say in response. It wasn't worth the energy to correct her and say, "Well, to be accurate, I'm a second-generation Indian *American*, and my husband is a second-gen Mexican *American*. Those terms mean a lot to me. They represent the complexity of my identity, and I like to be properly understood." But I didn't mention this because this whole introduction is odd to begin with. I don't go around introducing white people to my friends of color by saying, "This is Sarah. She's Anglo American," or "I want you to meet my friend Mike. He's white."

People only say things like this when they're looking for acknowledgment, as if they deserve an award. It's as if verbalizing someone's ethnicity and getting it right earns them points. That's what it felt like. This woman never came out and said it, but I'm pretty sure she was hoping I would be grateful to her for making my cultural identity hypervisible. But I wasn't. At all. I would have much preferred she mention something about where we first met or something we'd done together. You know, the way *normal* "friends" talk.

The way people talk to me or about me, or the way they introduce me to their friends, often conveys the idea that it's fun to run into me, *but in the same way that it's fun to go to the zoo every once in a while.* I feel like an object, like I'm being used as a prop in their story, and not like a real person. Perhaps they're hoping to get some interesting stories out of me or learn something new, but then the introduction is quickly followed by the polite goodbye, and I never see them again. I function as a substitute for real engagement with people on the east side and people of color in general. Two minutes of chitchat with me is all the satisfaction one needs to feel woke or "passionate about diversity." But I don't get the sense that they want to have a real friendship with me. People like this just enjoy knowing that I, as a person of color, exist tangentially in their life, and then they go about their day in their safe and comfortable community.

I don't want to be a mark on somebody's diversity checklist. My life doesn't exist to make yours feel more complete. People who treat me this way may call me their friend, but I wouldn't call them mine.

The Problem of Cultural Comfort Zones

When we are interacting with people of another culture, many of us correlate successful engagement with simply not being mean to them. And that's a good start. But that really is the lowest standard you can have and still have a positive interaction. It requires almost nothing on our part, yet everything is on the other person. We tell ourselves, "I'm open to meeting new people," but built into this approach is an expectation that people should come to us and do the heavy lifting in the relationship. If we're serious about pursuing deep and meaningful cross-cultural relationships, we need to put in a bit more work.

We can't just live in our own lane and interact when someone different from us happens to occasionally show up where we live. Instead, we need to step outside our cultural comfort zones and go to where people are at. We need to initiate.

Most of us don't like doing this. Whether we're Brown, Black, or white, we like staying in our bubble and doing things with other people like us. The whole point of a cultural comfort zone is the construction of mental security. By definition it is comfortable, a space where our activities and behaviors fit a routine and pattern that minimizes stress and risk.[1] It's our happy space, where we feel like we can be ourselves. And making friends with other people on our turf is always easier.

The problem is that most of the time our cultural comfort zones equate to monocultural communities. Think about your neighborhood, your favorite coffee shop, your school, your go-to grocery store, your workplace, your church, or your local park. In these places, if everyone looks like you, talks like you, and is in the same socioeconomic bracket as you, it's most likely a cultural comfort zone. If everyone enjoys the same activities, throws parties in the same way, and has the same views on friendships, politics, marriage, and punctuality, you are living in a cultural comfort zone. If everyone in your sphere listens to the same pastors and theologians, reads the same books, does the same Bible studies, and watches the same news channel, it's definitely a cultural comfort zone.

I'm not here to bash cultural comfort zones or monocultural communities. There's nothing inherently wrong with a white neighborhood or a Black neighborhood or a Brown neighborhood. I'm not trying to wholesale label the community you live in as good or bad. These kinds of spaces are simply part of our natural state—and there can be beauty in these cultural communities too. But as a follower of Jesus, you have a mandate to make friends with people of other cultures. It's one the most important changes you can make in your life in pursuit of the vision Jesus has for this world.[2] And if you want to do this, you're going to have to step outside your cultural comfort zone intentionally.

I want to add a caveat here, because a community can be multiethnic and still be monocultural. Multiethnic does not automatically translate to multicultural. You might live in a neighborhood or attend a church or be part of a workforce with multiple skin colors present, but if you are all middle class, the odds are that you share more cultural values than differences. Remember that culture, at its core, is a set of stories, and typically, people of similar socioeconomic brackets end up merging their narratives together. This is especially true for wealthy communities, which is where TV shows like *Black-ish* find their comedic edge. The family in this show, if you have never seen it, has lost some of its traditional African values precisely *because* they are middle class.

So when I suggest you need to step outside your monocultural community, I don't mean finding someone of a different skin color who happens to live next door to you. I mean finding people with real cultural differences from you.

This involves searching out people who hold different values, people who see the world differently than you. When these people do something, your first response will probably be: "Well, I wouldn't have done it that way."

Find *those* people and make friends with them.

Having friends of the same cultural background will always be easier. We don't have to switch gears, and we can just be ourselves. There's stability and reassurance in these relationships. But this same comfortability can lead to stagnancy when we get *too* comfortable. We lose the sense of urgency that drives us to meet new people. We become apathetic to the distance that lies between ourselves and other cultural groups. Or we let our imaginations get the best of us and start to fear people we don't come into regular contact with.

Many white people feel like they're in danger around Black- or Brown-skinned people, and it's this feeling of discomfort that leads them to label communities of color as dangerous. It's not necessarily because the crime rate is high, but simply because the people look different. I once told a white woman that I lived on the east side of Austin, and she instantly said: "Oh my gosh. That's the barrio. I would *never* go there." *Barrio* is a Spanish word that simply means neighborhood, but when white people use this term, it comes with an implication that it's a ghetto—a bad place that looks different from our own neighborhood with people of different skin colors and socioeconomic backgrounds. If you feel this way, you need to own that and work on deconstructing your fear. As author and social work professor Brené Brown explains, one of the worst things we can do is pretend our fear and uncertainty do not exist.[3] Just because we are nervous or scared doesn't mean we should ignore those feelings. We should fight to deconstruct our racial prejudices and lean into the discomfort we feel. Increasing our contact with another culture creates a context in which our racial prejudices and false ideas of the other can be challenged and corrected.[4]

If we want to begin the hard work of forming real cross-cultural friendships in which we don't make everything about ourselves, we have to break out of our routines, comfort zones, and monocultural spaces to explore uncharted territory.

Finding New Spaces

If we truly want to "become all things to all people" as Paul writes in 1 Corinthians 9:22, then we need to value the recovery of place as a theological category. For Paul, connecting with people across cultural divisions isn't purely for the sake of a conversion experience.[5] Paul chooses to leave a safe and comfortable cultural space because he recognizes that people's narratives and identities are tied to their sense of place, and caring for them means spending time in *their* location and valuing *their* community.

American theologian Willie James Jennings explains that humans are part of a story of place. God always intended for the earth to be a "signifier of identities," and specifically our cultural identities.[6] However, as Jennings argues, throughout the course of history Christians have ranked bodies and places according to their capacity for productivity rather than as a reflection of their unique participation in creation. Our preference for racial identities has reimagined people in terms of their marketplace value instead of understanding identity, landscape, and people in terms of a matrix of mutually informative relationships between spaces and bodies. Old Testament theologian Walter Brueggemann reinforces the importance of place in *The Land*: "Place is space which has historical meanings, where some things have happened which are now remembered, and which provide continuity and identity across generations. Place is a space in which important words have been spoken which have established identity, defined vocation, and envisioned destiny. Place is a space in which vows have been exchanged, promises have been made, and demands have been issued."[7] Who we are and where we live are inextricably linked. And as followers of Jesus, we need to value people of other cultures and their unique locales without placing value judgments on their communities or assessing them based on how their community benefits us.

We are placed peoples, influenced by our rootedness and the spaces we inhabit.[8] This is why Paul physically engages with people on their own turf. He doesn't learn about different people groups by reading a book about them or watching a documentary. He goes to them, talks with them, observes them, and spends time in their midst. He acquires firsthand knowledge and experience by walking their streets, and this is something we must learn to do as well. This is not something we can rush. There should be a slowness to our pace and an earnest desire to stop and get to know the people around us. We should want to genuinely know about the lives of the people across town. We should want to know where they shop and eat and play. We should step into their spaces in order to see them, experience life beside them, and understand what life is like through their eyes, as much as we can.

One of the great paradoxes of the twenty-first century is that we have instant connection with others at our fingertips through social media, and many of us live in close proximity, experiencing the hustle and bustle of urban spaces, yet we still feel separated from one another. We detach ourselves from real people and real places outside of our neighborhood and circle of friends. But when we choose to wander outside our immediate circles, we begin to experience a broader sense of community. We can begin to feel "at home" anywhere—and with anyone.

In the Gospels, Jesus is the Christ who wanders. He is seldom still, continually encountering others in unexpected contexts. He meets lonely women at wells, talks with children, and eats in the homes of tax collectors, who were seen to be sinners, living far from God. Jesus leaves the hustle and bustle of busy city centers and visits the cliffs. He goes to places filled with people the world has rejected. Jesus seeks people out, he loves them, and he eats with them. In doing so he makes it abundantly clear that every person in every context is worth his love and attention. His love and message of salvation are available to all, and he models this by physically visiting all sorts of different people.

Jesus, the wanderer, is our example. We need to show the world that as followers of Jesus we are not limited to a particular context. We should never communicate to people that our love for them is conditional based on whether they attend our church or live on a certain side of town. In emulating Christ, we must understand that Jesus was continually on the move. He entered our world in a specific time, place, and body. He changed who he was and came to us. We too need to be willing to change who we are to meet others where they live.

Just so we're clear, I'm not talking about signing up for an overseas mission trip. Traveling across an ocean is not the only way to encounter other cultures, and it's not even the best way. It is hard for me to understand how so many people can justify trips like this when the nations are now our neighbors. For most people in the United States, you don't have to travel far from your own driveway to meet someone of a different culture. Getting out of your cultural comfort zone doesn't require a two-week trip to Africa. It means visiting some neighborhoods you've been avoiding in the radius of your own city.

Jesus travels all the time during his ministry years, but he never goes very far. He travels from Nazareth to Jerusalem, to Samaria, around the regions bordering the Sea of Galilee, and even spends time in Egypt during his youth. Most of his travel is within a fifty-mile radius. Jesus doesn't go very far, but his reach is incredibly wide. Or consider the places the apostle Paul goes on his travels. Paul visits synagogues to meet with other Jews and goes to the town square to talk with Gentiles. He talks with people in the marketplace, by the river (Acts 16:12–15), and in prison (Acts 16:25–40). He visits people in their homes, including Aquila and Priscilla (Acts 18:1–3) and Titius Justus (Acts 18:7). He visits both Jewish and Greek academic schools (Acts 19:9–10). Paul knows the demographics of the cities he visits and lives in, and, like Jesus, he is a man who wanders in order to meet people right where they are.

Even more, Paul's movements are comprehensive. This is hinted at in his use of the word *all* in 1 Corinthians 9:19–23. Paul becomes all things to all people by seeking out every demographic within the societies he enters. No one is excluded or overlooked. No one occupies too low a standing or too high a position. Instead, every ethnic group that Paul encounters on his travels is worthy of his attention.[9] He doesn't bypass any people group based on their ethnicity. He is an apostle to all.

Like the people in Scripture, we cannot afford to live cloistered away. In the early church, Peter, Paul, and so many other male and female disciples are willing to move beyond their personal comfort zones and reach people where they are. New friendships begin when we put ourselves in new spaces, constantly going to different places for the single purpose of connecting with all people everywhere. It's plain and simple: you will not be able to make friends with people of other cultures unless you go to them.

Change It Up

We must choose to love people with their homes, streets, and communities in mind. This means breaking from our stable and comforting routines, changing the spaces we inhabit, and stepping into places that feel uncomfortable. Only when we are actively seeking people different from us will we find them. Here are a couple of suggestions for getting started.

Change Your Routine

Start by changing your routine. Think of all the places you normally drink coffee, go for walks, exercise, shop for groceries, watch movies, get your hair cut, and hang out. Now, consider how you might change this up to spend time in spaces that are culturally different from your norm. This may be easier if you live in an urban context, but even small towns and suburbs are more diverse than you might realize. If you don't know the ethnic demographics of your community, find out and make an intentional effort to seek out ethnic minorities. This is about learning to interrupt our normal patterns.

Making the journey from your culture into someone else's will stretch you emotionally, spiritually, and physically. Breaking from your monocultural space will also come with a degree of culture shock.[10] You'll experience a sense of confusion and disorientation as you try to navigate the aisles, sidewalks, and pews of a different cultural environment. When you step out, you'll need to get past the fact that you may be the only white person in an all-Black space. Or you'll need to embrace the discomfort of being the only African American in an all-Korean American space, or the only Indian American in an all-Mexican American space. Press on anyway. Discomfort cannot be an excuse for avoiding connection with people outside our cultural contexts.

Consider taking your kids to a playground in a different part of town where they'll rub shoulders with children of other ethnicities. It's important for them to hear kids speak Spanish (or Mandarin or Telugu) so it becomes normalized for them instead of "that foreign language" you hear once in a while. Drive to a park on the other side of town. Shop at a grocery store that's not convenient. Attend a church where you and your family are the minority. Sit and have coffee at a shop where you won't hear English. And while you are there, talk to people, smile, say hi, and find a way to make friends. The more you step outside your monocultural spaces, the easier it will get. In fact, the more you step out of your comfort zone in general, the more it will become normal to you, and you'll be able to stretch farther as you develop cultural flexibility.

Granted, saying hello to someone is just the tip of the iceberg. That's the beginning. If you can't even smile and greet a person of a different skin color on the sidewalk, that's a problem. If you only ever say hello, you will never move beyond surface-level relationships. And relationships are the real goal, right? We should inconvenience ourselves and travel down new roads to connect with people who are different from us.

I'm glad if you like Chinese food, but ordering takeout from a Chinese restaurant on special occasions or occasionally shopping at a local Asian store isn't going to cut it. You can go every week to a Mexican restaurant, eat their tacos, and never make a Mexican American friend. The goal is more than just surface-level engagement, more than simply learning or experiencing something new. The goal is to show real people of different cultures that you value them—their stories, their joys, their pain—and that you want to become their friend. We wander into new cultural spaces with the intent of building friendships so that lives can interweave and pieces of our everyday can begin to overlap with one another.

Change Where You Eat

Do you know what I long to hear after meeting someone from a different culture? Nothing means more to me than an invitation to have my family over for dinner to get to know each other better. Truly, I can't think of a better way to extend conversations and friendships than in homes at dinner tables, gathered around food.

Eating together is about more than just the food. Gathering around a table is a practice of solidarity, a declaration that we are committed to overcoming barriers of difference and division together. It is a choice to partake in an act that is both personal and intimate. You can't help but become more aware of who you are and *with whom* you are while gathered around a meal.[11] The dinner table is where we forge bonds over conversations that tap into our deeper longings for love, acceptance, and belonging. Do you want to build lifelong friendships? Start eating with people of other cultures. Want to move beyond "How was your week?" in your conversations? Break bread in each other's homes.

It takes courage to ask an acquaintance, or even a stranger, if they'd like to come over to your house for a meal. You must be willing to try something new when you invite a classmate, family at the park, or couple at church to share food with you. But it can be as simple as walking up to someone and saying four small words: "Want to eat together?" Practice turning this phrase into a habit. Your litmus test is whether you find yourself regularly asking people this question and find your weeks filling up with communal meals.

Don't just make them come to you. Be willing to go to *their* home and eat *their* food. Jesus and Paul always make it a point to eat with people where they live. Jesus literally tells people, "I'm coming to your house today." Why? Becoming all things to all people means that we aren't always the host. We need to be the guest at a new table filled with unknown spices and smells where listening and learning are our only motives. It may seem odd at first, but inviting yourself to another person's home is a form of reverse hospitality that's welcome and appreciated in many cultures. And it has the potential to connote respect and communicate equality toward the person you are seeking to connect with. In becoming the guest you will be more cognizant of what is most important in your host's life—family, friends, journeys, and memories.

Can it be difficult to go to other people's homes? Absolutely. You never know if your kids are going to behave nicely or have a complete meltdown. Different smells, like incense, can be challenging to contend with, and there's occasionally the problem of cat hair. (I am extremely allergic to both and have come to believe that God invented allergy medication for situations like this.) Do I always like the food I'm eating? Most of the time I do, but sometimes not. I have an Indian palate and certain flavors (like fish sauce) make my stomach queasy. Barring health reasons (and a preference for gluten-free food doesn't count), I always eat what I'm served for the sake of the gospel and my new friendship. To develop cross-cultural friendships we need to escape our cultural comfort zones, lay down our preferences, and make ourselves available to those around us.

Around the table we can ask questions and learn what people love. What do you love about your neighborhood? What celebrations are big in this community? Who are the local heroes? What are your historic landmarks? What do you wish people understood about your neighborhood? We should learn about their pain too by asking questions like these: How has this neighborhood been impacted by segregation? What do racism and injustice look like on these streets? Whose lives have been lost? What do you wish could be restored?

These conversations are never just about gathering facts; they're about what these stories do to us—how they change our hearts and our minds. We must listen with openness, allowing other people's stories to engender love, empathy, and care within us so this new community of friends starts to feel more like home.

This is an invitation to recognize the importance of *place*. Begin to connect with people of other cultures and grow more in tune with the spaces they inhabit. Don't expect them to come to you. Instead, step outside the comfortable, search for people, and then—eat together! Slowly but surely your lives and worlds will begin to interweave.

Chapter 7

Redefine Fluency

"What if we invited our new neighbors to my birthday dinner?"

I was sitting at our kitchen table, rummaging through my homemade recipe book, and trying to decide which cake to make when my husband's question drifted over from the living room.

"Which ones?" I asked. "You mean the family from Myanmar?"

"Yeah!" came his response. "We need to get to know them better."

I couldn't have agreed more. Our new neighbors had moved in about a week ago, and we had tried, rather unsuccessfully, to introduce ourselves. The street had been packed with cars that day, with over thirty people coming and going through their front door. With my baby girl on my hip and my toddler by my side, we had walked across the yard past three men squatting in a row smoking. I smiled and said, "Hi," as their eyes silently observed our every movement. Most of the commotion was coming from the backyard, and we arrived just in time to watch a man singlehandedly scale a large oak tree with a machete between his teeth. No ropes. No ladders. When he reached the top, he wrapped his arm around one branch and systematically began chopping down the rest of the tree. It was the most impressive—and terrifying—thing I'd ever seen.

Several of the women smiled and waved at me, but when they didn't slow down or stop working, I thought to myself, "We should come back later."

Since that day, we'd been looking for the right opportunity to connect, and Aaron's upcoming birthday party seemed as good a time as any. So the following Saturday we fired up our grill, made a crazy amount of fajitas and guacamole, and walked back over and knocked on their door. There was no warning I was coming. No pretty invitation or formal introductions. My plan was just to talk to whoever opened the door. A woman who looked to be my age appeared, and I simply said: "Hi! I'm Michelle, your neighbor. We have fajitas because it's my husband's birthday! Want to eat dinner with us?"

The woman smiled and said something like, "Oh, oh." It quickly became clear she didn't speak much English, but no matter. I've spent most of my life in bilingual spaces and with more aunties and uncles than I can count who've never spoken a single word of English. I smiled back and began pointing at my house and making gestures of eating together. I'll spare you the details. It wasn't smooth or pretty. But something seemed to click. "Ah, you?" the woman replied with a nod, pointing in the same direction as my house.

"Yes! That's where I live!" I replied. "You come eat?"

"Okay, okay," she said.

She waved at me and shut the door.

I found myself standing before a closed door, wondering what had just happened. I stood there for a second, not sure what I should do. Did she understand what I had said? Should I knock and try again? After standing for a minute deliberating, I walked back to my house and told Aaron, "I *think* they're gonna come over." We started setting out plates, cups, and silverware just in case, all the while praying my words had made sense to our neighbors.

Sure enough, about ten minutes later, there was a knock at the front door.

The minute I opened it, I was greeted by ten people. There were men, women, and children of all ages, all smiling with their eyes on me. "Hello! Welcome!" I said, while also turning around and shouting in as friendly a tone as I could, "Aaron, can you come here, please?" I didn't know much about Myanmar, a country in Southeast Asia, but I know Indian culture, and I wanted my husband there to greet the men who had arrived.

Everyone took off their plastic flip-flops before coming inside, and that kicked off a beautiful night of fun and chaos. We never asked, but I was pretty sure everyone who came lived in that single house next door, a reality that is typical for many immigrant families. The kids never stopped running around, and there was a pickup game of soccer in our backyard within the first three minutes, with everyone playing barefoot. I had no idea which kid belonged to which adult.

Meanwhile, the men and women walked into our living room, stood silently in a row, and continued to smile at us. There was a split second as some of them clasped hands together and bowed when I wondered to myself: What on earth are we going to talk about? To be honest, I still wasn't sure if they knew this was Aaron's birthday party. But Aaron and I were determined to make this relationship work, regardless of the communication barriers between us.

Out back we had a huge spread of Mexican snacks and drinks. We spoke English; they spoke Burmese. There was a lot of pointing and gesturing, and sometimes we figured out what the other person was saying, but most of the time we were utterly clueless. But we just laughed and moved on. Even though we didn't always understand one another, the conversation seemed to flow. Good food, love, and laughter united us when language failed.

I don't think our guests had ever heard of tres leches cake or fideo. But they ate all the Mexican food we served them and loved it, and we loved their company. They learned Aaron was a pastor ("You, pastor?" "Yes, pastor!"), and we learned they were Burmese Christians ("Us, God, yes"). And before they left, we prayed together. Beyond that, we had no idea what their stories were, what they liked or disliked, what they'd gone through in coming to this country, or even why they had come to the United States. We didn't know how old they were, what they did for a living, or what their interests were. But we still found ways to communicate and connect, and we began laying the foundation for a deeper friendship.

Different, Different, Not Same

People will say they want to have friends from different cultures. But let's be real. It's hard. As a brown-skinned woman who's had *a lot* of people tell me they value diverse friendships, I've become skeptical over the years. Most of the time, what people really mean is that they want to know people who *look* different from them but who still *think* and *act* and *talk* the same way they do. There's a glimmer of hope that somehow a Korean man and a Mexican family will find something in common or that an Anglo American woman and a Native American woman will share some point of similarity that they can build from. In other words, we seek out friendships with the belief that, if we just dig deep enough, we will discover we're more similar than different. More than that, once we're able to connect with someone over shared worldviews, behaviors, or experiences, deep bonds will form.

But this gets complicated if we assume we will be able to uncover this connection with any person we meet. What happens if the person doesn't speak English? What happens when you don't know how to communicate with each other? What happens when you don't have the words to figure out their likes and dislikes, their favorite foods, or the story of their family? Languages are the gateways to people's cultures, and differences in languages usually point to differences in histories and experiences as well. If you can't connect on this basic level, then what? Do you just quit?

I have conversations with people about this topic all the time. I've done cross-cultural relationship trainings and seminars, and every time I mention that people of different cultures might not have things in common, there's always someone who disagrees with me. Someone once told me, "You might *think* you have nothing in common, but the more you get to know one another, you will realize you do have things in common." Her words implied that if we devote ourselves to learn about the other person, we will eventually discover points of commonality. Others have said, "I think that even if someone is from a different culture, it's always possible to find some common ground: motherhood, hobbies, literature, laughter, faith, nature. The possibilities for appreciating things together seem endless." The underlying assumption in these ideas is that there is always a possibility of sharing something in common and that this discovery is just around the corner, if you are persistent. This perspective also echoes the traditional advice in most friendship books: similarity breeds connection.[1]

But there is a problem with this approach. It bases everything on finding common ground. And that indirectly implies that if you cannot find common ground with someone from a different culture, then you're off the hook. The friendship doesn't need to be pursued. It's just not going to work; better luck next time! If we approach friendship looking only for points of connection, then when people check that box, we happily become friends. But if those points of connection do not materialize, we feel free to part ways. Even worse, the pursuit of common ground as the basis for friendship risks basing the relationship on ourselves, on our likes, dislikes, wants, and needs. We are dangerously close to wanting friendship with people of other ethnicities and cultures only if they are just like us, at the very least if they speak the same language.

That's the real problem. There is nothing wrong with looking for common ground, but *overemphasizing* the need for commonality leads to a skewed foundation for cross-cultural friendships. It creates false expectations of what it should be like to connect, particularly with non-English speakers. This can include immigrants and refugees who speak limited English, but it also includes men and women who have lived their entire lives in the United States and who still only speak Spanish, Tagalog, Vietnamese, Arabic, Korean, Mandarin, or Telugu. I have so many friends whose parents have come to live with them, and they spend most of their time in the home, watching their grandchildren. They have little opportunity to go out in public to meet new people and practice English. But these men and women need friends too, just like the rest of us. The language barriers may keep us from easily finding common ground, but this is an opportunity for us to listen and learn, to understand what life is like for them.

Unfortunately, many immigrants, refugees, and other non-English speakers end up on the losing end of relationships. They're the ones nobody notices. They are told, "Sorry, I don't know how to connect with you." They're rejected, abandoned, and tossed aside because they are too different. The obstacles to learning each other's histories, common values, and experiences feel insurmountable when we lack the common ground of a shared language. These barriers are often too difficult for the average person in the United States to overcome. The language divide is a broken wheel that has been turning around and around since the formation of our nation.[2]

What can we do? Rather than giving up when language is a barrier, we'll need to learn how to connect with people— including immigrants and refugees—even when the basic elements of shared language and social cues are absent.

No Barrier Is Too Great

In the first-century world, the dominant language and culture of the day was Greco-Roman. Those who did not speak Greek or live according to the Greco-Roman norms were known as barbarians and Scythians. These two people groups lived disconnected from the majority culture.[3] Relative to Rome, they were from faraway places, and people of the Roman Empire had limited contact with them. The noun *barbarian* only appears six times in the New Testament, and one of those instances is found in 1 Corinthians 14:11: "If then I do not grasp the meaning of what someone is saying, I am a *foreigner* to the speaker, and the speaker is a *foreigner* to me" (emphasis added). The word *foreigner* is an English translation of the Greek *barbaros*, which is where we get the word *barbarian*.[4] In the first century, the word was synonymous with someone who spoke a language other than Greek, someone who was generally unintelligible to outsiders.

Based on descriptions of barbarians in the New Testament, we know that even in the first-century people who were different—who spoke a different language—were viewed as less likable *because* they spoke a different language. The Scythians, who are referenced in Scripture alongside the barbarians, were a people group made up of tribes north of the Black Sea. They were considered an extreme example of barbarians, the worst kind of foreigner. Among the educated urban elite of the Greco-Roman world, who saw all people as either Greek (educated citizen) or barbarian (uncivilized foreigner), the term *Scythian* came to epitomize everything negative about foreign barbarians. Barbarians and Scythians were the ultimate outsiders, with different languages, customs, values, and social dynamics. They did not even fit the acceptable majority-minority divide within society. Both Jews and Greeks ostracized them. The Jews were an acceptable minority within the Greco-Roman world, but the barbarians and Scythians were despised. They were the outliers with no place in society.

This way of labeling and cataloging people is still around today. Each of us have certain cultural groups we consider acceptable, and others that make us less comfortable. We all have people in our lives whom we treat as barbarians and Scythians. These are the people who don't fall under the typical black-white divide in our society or into acceptable minority categories. They are the immigrants, the refugees, and anyone else who doesn't speak English. They are the people in our country who don't identify with our national culture, who are unacculturated, and who are visibly perceived as "other."

Does the Bible have anything to say to us about how we treat these people? While Paul focuses the conversation on cultural accommodation to Jews and Gentiles in 1 Corinthians 9:19–23, he expands his list in Colossians 3:11 to include the outsider and the foreigner. He writes, "Here there is no Gentile or Jew, circumcised or uncircumcised, barbarian, Scythian, slave or free, but Christ is all, and is in all." In other words, Paul refers to "foreign-language speakers" in these verses, reminding followers of Jesus that we should not impose divisions where Christ has united us. We must learn to accommodate to everyone, and this includes those we have difficulty communicating with. We need to learn how to adapt and transform for those who don't identify with our national language, culture, and norms.

This mandate is incredibly timely. We've all seen how harmless differences between people of different nationalities can quickly snowball into distrust, prejudice, and hostility. Research tells us how, historically, nationals feel threatened culturally by those perceived as foreigners.[5] When people are asked to consider sharing a community with people who speak a different language, they often respond with negative emotions. Linguistic differences can provoke fear and hostility, and there is a sad and wrong perception that outsiders pollute our national culture with different languages. Some respond to this threat with vitriol and aggression, blaming non-English speakers for societal problems—a reality that led to the rise of anti-Asian racism during the time of COVID-19. We convince ourselves that non-English speakers are taking our jobs, increasing the crime rates in our neighborhoods, and jeopardizing our religious freedoms. So we tell ourselves they should be sent back to where they came from ("Go home!"),

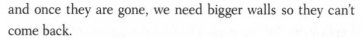

and once they are gone, we need bigger walls so they can't come back.

How do we stop seeing non-English speakers as threats? We embrace change for the sake of Christ. Instead of seeing new languages—and the new customs and lifestyles that accompany them—as disrupters to our way of life, we view them as teachers and guides for our own transformation. In Romans 1:14 Paul writes, "I am obligated both to Greeks and non-Greeks [that is, 'barbarians'], both to the wise and the foolish." Underlying these words by Paul is a comprehensive worldview for becoming all things to all people. Paul holds up the two most disparate groups in the known world of this time side by side—the Greeks and the barbarians. In doing so, he declares that he is committed to both. His love for Christ motivates him to serve every person, regardless of who they are and what they speak, and to meet them where they live. Paul is driven to come alongside them, getting to know them as valued human beings who have been created in God's image, and this includes the language they speak.[6] If we want to do this today, our language, our cultural expressions, and our modes of communication need to be flexible. We need to be open to change.

Paul puts this into practice in Acts 28. In one of the final stories in the book of Acts, Paul is shipwrecked on the island of Malta, and he meets the islanders. These people are immediately identified as "barbarians." Verses 1 and 2 set the scene: "Once safely on shore, we found out that the island was called Malta. The islanders ['barbarians'] showed us unusual kindness. They built a fire and welcomed us all because it was raining and cold." Everything about this scene has profound implications for our lives. The first description of these barbarians notes their "unusual kindness," a bold gesture pointing to God's providence and protection over the lives of Paul and his companions after a rough journey. It also highlights one of the most highly regarded virtues of antiquity—the virtue of hospitality—and makes this a tale about the kindness of strangers.[7] These non-Greek speakers are no less polished, smart, or civilized than anyone else. Rather, they are good, loving people who receive Paul and his shipmates and welcome them. The word *welcome* in these verses implies both shelter and hospitality. Remember, Paul had been shipwrecked, and he and his shipmates would have been chilled and drenched and in need of warmth. The barbarians make them a fire and tend to their immediate needs. Luke, the author of this story, sets the barbarians up as an example for followers of Jesus. Like the barbarians, we should practice hospitality. Translated to our culture today, we can learn much from the foreigner and the immigrant—kindness and hospitality included.

Paul and the barbarians don't have the same native tongue. Perhaps they speak some broken Greek together, but we don't really know. The story doesn't mention them talking as they sit around the fire, yet they are still able to connect. There is unspoken power in our actions, and often in just being together. Paul isn't condescending; he doesn't demonize them. He is quiet, and this too is a radical act. It breaks from our traditional conception of what a cross-cultural connection should look like. Sometimes just being together is enough. Fellowship in silence can have depth and meaning, and more importantly, as Paul demonstrates in Acts 28, it means that no one is beyond connection. Even if you do not speak the same language, no matter your nationality, culture, or background, no barrier is too great for connection.

A New Way to Communicate

There will always be some people and cultures that are harder to connect with than others, and building relationships will require some outside-the-box ideas. I'd like to suggest a few ways we can connect with others, even when we do not share a common language or culture.

Believe in the Power of Silence

As we saw with Paul on the island of Malta, we don't need to fear silence. Instead, we should embrace it. Many of us have a compulsion to constantly fill every void with words, and this creates a false understanding of the role communication should play in relationships. If we place a premium on constant, unending conversation, then is it any wonder that we don't value relationships with people who don't speak our language? It's time to flip the script. We need to learn how to forge relationships without words as the primary connector.

Language is defined as a system of verbal *and* nonverbal symbols used to communicate,[8] and this means that not every connection must rely on words. There is power in embracing conversational silence and simply choosing to be present. You can form bonds through shared activities like cooking, eating, and enjoying special moments together. There is nothing wrong with verbal communication, of course, but we should resist the pressure to talk the entire time. You can make gestures, point at things, and laugh together. And while there will be much that is "unsaid," the silence that remains should be welcomed as part of your relationship. Acknowledge it, accept it, and embrace it in order to show that you are relaxed enough in each other's company to enjoy quiet moments together.

I know this is a radical idea for some of us. You may never have thought of silence as a tool for connection with others. Yet silence can function as an equalizer in unequal relationships. Instead of constantly talking past each other, you'll just be two people committed to spending time in each other's presence purely to appreciate the other person as they are. Status, values, attitudes, and beliefs won't be at the fore of your conscience, and they certainly won't be driving your ability to connect. The only thing left will be enjoying someone for who they are, a person made in the image of God, instead of what they can offer to you.

Embrace Ambiguity

We also need to embrace ambiguity in communication. When a person speaks to you in a different language, instead of responding, "Hang on—I don't know that word. Let me check Google Translate," show a willingness to sit and listen. Let new words wash over you, even if you don't understand their meaning. Admittedly, that's no easy task.

Most of us hate ambiguity. We want to make sense of the world and have a strong need to know and understand what is going on around us. As social psychologist and public theologian Christena Cleveland puts it, this is largely because "if we understand the world around us, we have a far greater chance of controlling it."[9] Scrutinizing every word that comes out of someone's mouth allows us to direct conversations, to make sure people see us the way we want to be seen, and to determine certain outcomes. When another language is at play, we are rendered powerless. We can't maintain the conversation, let alone fully understand it. As a result, we go to great lengths to avoid this ambiguity, which translates to avoiding non-English speakers.[10]

We should not take lightly the impact of choosing to avoid someone of a different culture. The barrier of language has led to a new kind of segregation. Non-English speakers in our country are often placed in separate and unequal groups. Consider, for example, Spanish-speaking services at mega-churches and separate Bible study classes for immigrants. In fact, discrimination can often be masked by the language excuse. For those who believe English is the superior language, it becomes permissible to discriminate against fellow citizens who don't speak like they do. This has been statistically proven in school systems where gifted Spanish-speaking students are placed in programs separate from then their white peers.[11] Immigrants who don't speak English face discrimination in the workplace and in the job market. People often don't even want to listen to a speaker or teacher with an accent, claiming they can't understand what they're saying and rendering their message less valuable. Rather than avoiding this, we need to begin deconstructing the belief that people who don't speak English are less smart or talented than we are. We need to figure out how a confluence of languages can flourish in one setting and start learning that it's okay not to always understand the conversation.

Body language can communicate a lot. Concepts and emotions can be expressed through gestures, expressions, postures, and eye movements. When words are absent,[12] we should attend to nonverbal communication efforts as much as possible. We need to grow in our tolerance for ambiguity, training ourselves to find unfamiliar situations exciting rather than frightening, and learning that conversations don't always need closure. In these contexts, the rules will be less clear, and the engagement will feel far less organized. You won't know where things will lead or what the other person will think of you. The few words they speak to you in English might come across as harsh or too direct, and you're going to have to accept that they might mean something *other* than what you are hearing. We shouldn't get frustrated when we can't fully understand what they're saying. That will immediately communicate that you don't value that person for who they are.

Growing in our tolerance for ambiguity leads to a greater capacity for optimism. If we learn to go beyond entry-level conversations on food and the weather and can embrace ambiguity in those deeper conversations about faith, families, politics, social issues, and more, we will be laying a solid foundation for lasting connections with non-English speakers.

Learn New Languages

Finally, instead of expecting people to speak English, learn the basic elements of their language. Culturally accommodating to non-English speakers means focusing on them and valuing both what and how they speak. Learning other languages is how we show others that we see something beautiful in their words, modes of communication, and cultural expression. More than that, being comfortable enough to have a conversation with someone in a language besides English builds trust. A person who speaks Bulgarian, Spanish, Thai, or Swahili as their first language will not feel cared for if there is no space for them to express themselves in their own tongue. We shouldn't expect them to speak English. Language plays such an important role in a person's cultural identity, and when we adapt to those around us, we honor them.

Language shapes a person's perceptions, thoughts, and view of reality. Language is more than a by-product of culture or a tool to communicate. Language informs self-understanding—our perception of what is real and true. Words make sense of the world. This implies that if you don't learn another person's heart language, you're not fully adapting yourself to understand them and their culture. More than that, learning languages can change your personality. Research has long shown that learning a new language will lead to changes in our attitudes, feelings, and behaviors—and these are changes we should embrace.

Learning new languages should be pursued at both individual and organizational levels. Sit down and ask the person you're befriending to teach you what to say and when. Practice, practice, and practice some more. Make it a point to learn a new sentence each week (or every two weeks if languages aren't your thing). If more than one language is spoken in your church, make it a point to reflect the linguistic diversity of your church members in the Sunday morning liturgy, in the reading of Scripture, in sermons, in discipleship resources, and in other forms of communication—and, most importantly, let the people who speak those languages guide and direct these initiatives. Translations should be made available as widely as possible. Policies and procedures should be translated into whatever languages are spoken in the workplace. Bosses should attempt to learn the language of their workers as a way to show them they are valued.

I'm not saying you have to master five different languages perfectly. It's not about how proficient your linguistic abilities are but rather your willingness to change how you communicate. It's about being willing to lean into a new language, to study body gestures, tones, and cultural expressions and to internalize them as much as you can. It's about allowing new words and phrases to change how you think and act, to become more like a Chinese immigrant or a Venezuelan refugee, for example, in the way you move your head, hold your body, and use your eyes.

Granted, what I've said elsewhere in this book still rings true. If you don't know Hindi and don't have any Indian friends, then don't try to say, "Namaste," at an Indian restaurant and hope your waiter will be impressed. That's still awkward and perhaps even offensive. When I say learn new languages, I'm talking about it within the context of real relationships, with people you love and care about and are trying to truly connect with. In Chicago, Aaron and I had a number of Persian friends who spoke Farsi. Each time we went over for a meal, we'd ask them to teach us new words; their greetings and farewells, how to say please and thank you, and useful phrases for basic conversation. They gladly taught us, and we would make it a point to remember and repeat them as often as we could. That was but one small way that we showed our Persian neighbors how much we loved them.

A lot is involved in communicating across cultures. Fluency should be determined by the level of connection being made, not the perfection of the language spoken or translated. We need to set different rubrics for successful communication and learn to accommodate to the people around us by becoming more fluid and flexible, willing to learn new things as we seek to love others.

Chapter 8

Change Your Perspective on Justice

"Oh, um, would you excuse me for a sec?" I asked as my phone buzzed again. "I need to—relay something to my husband."

My friend nodded and continued to sip her coffee as I proceeded to rush out the front door of the coffee shop. "Pick up . . . pick up," I said to myself as I impatiently listened to the ringing, hoping Aaron would answer. My heart felt like it was beating its way out of my chest, and every second created a greater sense of impending disaster.

I had received one of those texts that, no matter where you are, you just can't ignore. It's the kind that screams, "Stop everything you're doing and deal with this before it becomes a runaway train." Little did Aaron and I know that a church announcement about an upcoming conference on immigrants would anger a good number of Christians in our city. The graphic had only been up for a few hours, and already I was starting to see dozens of texts, posts, and tweets from fellow Christians, even friends, who were speaking against it.

There was nothing insulting or crude in the language we had used. We simply said we were going to host an event to highlight the stories of our immigrant neighbors and Dreamers in particular. We are a minority-led multicultural church where over 50 percent of our congregants are Latino, several of whom are also undocumented. My husband himself is second-generation Mexican American. Ministry for us involves caring for the immigrants in our midst, helping them find jobs, making sure their kids have food to eat, living life together, and mourning together after ICE raids or when families have been separated. In many gatherings over coffee and pan dulce and dinners around tables, we have listened to our immigrant church members express a longing for their stories to be heard.

"We want people to know the truth about us," one woman told us.

So Aaron and I started thinking about ways to amplify their voices. We believe in narrative justice and empowering the voiceless to speak for themselves.[1] Much of the conversation on immigrants and border crossings in this country is steered by dominant, majority voices. But justice in this conversation should mean listening to *all* the voices. It means taking the mic away from those speaking loudest to amplify the voices of those at the margins of society. Telling your own story is a God-given right. Every person of every cultural background and heritage has the right to talk about their experiences, struggles, and joys. Everyone has the right to be

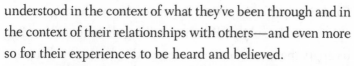

understood in the context of what they've been through and in the context of their relationships with others—and even more so for their experiences to be heard and believed.

Pastor Ken Wytsma writes, "One of the things I've realized and begun to teach is that the message is not only in the content of *what* is being taught or presented but also in *who* is bringing it. Indeed, when we address injustices and fight for the oppressed, we can fall into suppressing those we seek to liberate by failing either to shift the power dynamic or to recognize the need for promoting the first-person voice of the oppressed."[2] This is exactly what narrative justice is all about.

Aaron and I were seeking to bring narrative justice to the immigrant community in Austin. Yet the minute the announcement for the conference went out, the pushback began. There were angry Christians in our city who thought loving immigrants was a violation of their biblical morals to separate church and politics. Some viewed unauthorized immigrants in our country as nothing more than criminals. For them, justice is not about holistic care, as we see in Scripture. It's a matter of law and order, crime and punishment. These people broke the law, so we need to send them back to wherever they came from. Isn't that what Romans 13 requires, obedience to government laws? I kid you not, friends reached out to us that following week, letting us know that pastors were telling their congregants not to attend our conference.

Honestly, it was hard to hear those words. I can understand people disagreeing and wanting to reach out and have a conversation. They could say something like, "I disagree with what you're doing, and here's why . . ." I can even understand

Christians preferring to just stay neutral or not having a strong opinion on the subject. But those talking about us and sending us angry messages were not interested in having civil conversations. There was name-calling and words I cannot repeat. There was an accusation that we weren't true Christians if we did something like this. My personal favorite insult: we must be liberal Democrats.

My greatest frustration, though, wasn't the attacks themselves. I've had those before. What frustrated me most was *who* was sending the messages. These were people with very strong opinions on immigration who didn't know a single immigrant personally. Most of the angry Christians virtually shouting at us didn't know the single immigrant woman in our church with three kids who has led a very hard life. Her parents brought her to Florida when she was fourteen and basically abandoned her there. Left alone on the streets, she had to fend for herself and ultimately met a guy and got pregnant. Then the two of them moved here to Austin where they had two more children before he abandoned her too. Now, this woman has no documentation. She isn't in the system, and she isn't eligible for a driver's license, a work permit, or even medical insurance. She's alone, helpless, and vulnerable and has three kids to care for and feed. She's not a criminal; she is someone to love and befriend. Imagine how *she* felt hearing that prominent white churches in our city were telling their congregants they shouldn't listen to her story.

We also quickly realized that many of the people angry with us didn't know anything about the Deferred Action for Childhood Arrivals (DACA) policy or even who Dreamers were. I remember a conversation with a fellow Christian leader on the west side of town a week before the conference. He sat there glaring at me with his arms folded over his chest as I tried to give him the backstory for the conference. But when I asked to share some of the statistics about DACA recipients in our city with him, his posture immediately changed. He awkwardly shuffled his legs and looked down with a confused expression on his face. "What is DACA?" he asked.

I couldn't believe my ears. This man had come ready to pick a fight with me on my biblical stance toward immigration yet didn't even know the basic facts of immigration today. I was ready to explode. He didn't know any immigrants personally. I'm pretty sure he didn't have any immigrants, let alone Dreamers, in his church. How did I know? Because these are the 101-level conversations you have with your immigrant friends and neighbors. He wasn't educated on the subject and had likely heard what he wanted to hear from his favorite news channel. That's never enough. Fear and ignorance were guiding his response.

I spent the rest of our conversation not talking about the conference but mapping out the facts about DACA and Dreamers, dispelling myths, and talking about why Christians should care for immigrants. Things went in a more positive direction after that, but I remain unsettled by that experience because what happened that day is a microcosm of the sentiments and views of many Christians. They have immediate—and often angry—responses to the big issues of our day, issues and concerns related to race and culture like immigration, police brutality, and racism. But they rarely have any friends who are directly impacted by the issue. It's not personal for them. It's not impacting their family or their community. They may not have all the facts, even though they think they do, and they assert their claims with ignorance reinforced by privilege. Even worse, their objections can be damaging to the vulnerable in our society.

That has to stop.

Stop Being Selfish

We are easily mobilized to speak out about the things that impact us directly, the things we care about. If you are a conservative, you might not need to be convinced to participate in the March for Life or to vote for politicians who stand against abortion. But if someone were to ask you to stand up for the minorities in your city, to protest alongside them to highlight the pain in their community and to amplify their voices, would you do it?

Seriously. Think about it.

If we're being honest with ourselves, many of us have a knee-jerk reaction to issues that do not directly impact us. While this happens between white Christians and people of color, it also happens between Asian American and African American communities. It happens between the Latino and Native American communities too. Most of the time we don't care about the problems happening in *other* people's communities. We consciously or unconsciously tout the mantra "If it's not happening to me, it's not important," or worse, "If it's not happening to me, it must not be true."

Asian Americans who talk about their experiences of racism during COVID-19 are called snowflakes.[3] The Black community cries out after the murder of a Black man by armed white civilians, and evangelicals question whether the boy is to blame. Native Americans plead to have conversations about things like stolen land, and we turn a blind eye. We're either disclaiming each other's statements or, in the words of Dr. Andrea Smith, competing in a silo of Olympic oppression to see who has suffered the most.[4]

I can't tell you how many Christians I've talked with who want to have friends of other cultures, but the minute I bring up the idea of lamenting over the death of yet another Black man, participating in a march against racism, speaking up against unjust policies and laws, or going to the border and caring for immigrants, their response changes. Some grow viscerally angry. Even though they don't have any friends from subdominant cultures, they want to educate *me* about the facts. Every time a Black man or woman is killed, white folks will come out in droves to say things like, "But not all white people are racist," or "But do you really know the facts?" or "Did you know they had a criminal record?" All the while, the Black community continues to suffer under the weight of grief and trauma over the loss of Botham Jean, Tamir Rice, Michael Brown, Trayvon Martin, Terrance Franklin, Philando Castile, De'Von Bailey, Walter Scott, Ahmaud Arbery, Breonna Taylor, and many others. Racism is so ingrained in our society that we are hardwired to harden our hearts when we hear about yet another shooting.

Instead of listening to the outcries of our minority

neighbors, many Christians have convinced themselves that taking action on behalf of the vulnerable is too worldly. Standing for Dreamers and raising our voices against the disappearance of indigenous women and girls are relegated to another "social agenda." It's all a ploy by liberals, progressives, and neo-Marxists, and we're not gonna touch those ideas with a ten-foot pole. Or it's seen as too political or unbiblical. When the call for Black Lives Matter rings out, instead of seeing the importance of that statement and hearing what is being said, many Christians try to mute the point by saying, "All Lives Matter."

We respond this way when things aren't personal. We don't get involved because we have little to no connection with the people whose situation we are dismissing or condemning. To be frank, this is selfish and wrong.

Become the Weak

We need a new starting point. Justice shouldn't be something we discuss from a singular point of view. We need to get out of our own heads. We need to step away from our history and our story and be willing to embrace other cultural groups and listen to others' stories, especially the stories of those who have been oppressed. In Scripture, those without power and those who have been oppressed are considered "the weak." In 1 Corinthians 9:22 Paul writes, "To the weak I became weak, to win the weak," What Paul is saying here is revolutionary. He is telling us that when it comes to caring for the weak (i.e., the poor and oppressed) in our society, we need to *become* them.

When we interpret the word *weak* within the context of the rest of 1 Corinthians, we see that it means a couple of things. Beginning in 1 Corinthians 1:27, Paul uses the term *weak* to contrast a group of people against those he considers arrogant.[5] This group included those in the church who were made to feel inferior because they were not exercising their rights in relation to the gifts of the Spirit such as wisdom or knowledge. But it also included people who had no status in the world's eyes—no power, no patronage, and no great wealth. These people were suffering at the hands of the elitists, and they were regarded by them as less than adequate because they didn't have many material possessions.[6] When Paul says, "God chose the foolish things of the world to shame the wise; God chose the weak things of the world to shame the strong" (1:27), he's creating a dichotomy between the strong and the weak, between those who have power and those who don't. More importantly, just as "God chose the lowly things of this world and the despised things" (1:28), Paul follows this pattern by personally choosing to *become* the weak and to lay down his power and privilege too.

Becoming the weak is a new and different charge from Paul, distinct from his commentary in 1 Corinthians 9:19–21 on becoming *like* Jews and Greeks. This is not just about learning how to appreciate and adapt to other people's cultural expressions, traditions, and lifestyles. When real problems of inequity and injustice are at stake, Paul says we need to step into these people's shoes and treat their problems as if they were our own. We need to address verbal, emotional, and physical attacks against a person of color through that person's eyes, not our own. We need to exercise solidarity, as Paul did, with the vulnerable by declaring, "I am weak," and then project our imagination into their world, doing our best to understand what they are experiencing.[7]

When we talk about the weak, we also have to think along racial lines. The division of the weak and the strong often has racial dynamics. There's just no getting around that. The subdominant groups are typically weak because they are the minority in that culture. This is not meant to be derogatory or suggest that they are inadequate in some way. It's simply a contrast with the arrogant (who are strong, often possessing greater power and privilege). By and large within human history, minority groups are more vulnerable, and I believe that if Paul were speaking to us today, he would demand that we give up status and power to care for people of color at the margins of society and make sure that exercising our rights isn't putting people of color in harm's way.

This isn't a liberal agenda. Paul's discourse on the dichotomy between the strong and the weak is important because it's a gospel issue. When the powerful abuse the weak, when the privileged trample over those who are powerless or fail to care for their pains as they suffer, it leads the weak to stumble. In James 5:1–6, for example, the rich are condemned for their mistreatment of poor day laborers. The author describes how the rich withhold equity and justice in the relationship and equates their inhumane actions to murder. The arrogance and disinterest of the rich not only harm the bodies and the livelihood of the poor *but also affect their acceptance of the gospel.* So Paul is willing to become all things, including becoming one of the weak, so that "by all possible means" he can save some (1 Cor. 9:22). If this is true, then disregarding the needs of the weak is akin to diminishing the gospel.

The message in 1 Corinthians 9:19–23 is a charge to Christians to do whatever it takes, without disobeying the law of Christ, to gain people for Christ, and this includes interrupting cycles of pain, oppression, and injustice in all its forms. We can only do this properly when we step into the shoes of those who are hurting. For us today this means taking on the mindset and identity of a person of color in this country. The only way you can become the weak is by learning to live like those who are disempowered and oppressed, seeing life through their eyes, mourning what they mourn, and fighting against systems of oppression as if they were your own.

This is the only healthy way forward. We must see the slogan Black Lives Matter as a Black man or woman sees it. We must understand the conversation on immigration from the lens of a single pregnant teen who has been abandoned at the border. We must approach the issue of missing indigenous women and girls as if we ourselves were Native American and our mother, daughter, or wife had gone missing. We also must approach the problem of racism through the lens of Black and Brown people, who repeatedly experience and witness violence against their communities and their personhood. It's about facing each issue and seeing it through the eyes of the weak—those who are directly affected.

If you are white, you will have to take off your white lens. If you have power and privilege, you will have to take off your lenses of privilege, power, and comfort and replace them with a lens that sees the world through the embodied lives and experiences of those on the margins. Make the issues that are important to minorities just as important to you. If you are a person of color, make the issues of other subdominant communities important to you as well. Understand the reasons behind their emotions and do everything possible to delve into their well of pain and trauma. Treat their pain as if it were your own, and verbally and physically respond the way they would.

See the World through Minority Eyes

To live your life as a communal minority is a continual act of cultural accommodation. There is no greater challenge than this. We have the capacity to do that. It is possible. But all of us have to exercise the necessary muscles. Here are some suggestions to get you started.

Let Minorities Lead the Conversation

In many of the stories in Scripture where someone is abused, assaulted, or oppressed, justice is rendered by allowing their story to be heard. God cares about our stories, and his commitment to narrative justice flows through the Scriptures. Consider, for example, the book of Judges. Here we read story after story of injustice, including the assault, rape, and murder of an unnamed woman in Judges 19. This is a horrific murder, and when the people of Israel learn of it, they shout, "We must do something! So speak up!" (v. 30). The heinous,

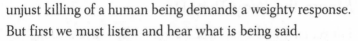

unjust killing of a human being demands a weighty response. But first we must listen and hear what is being said.

Becoming weak means relinquishing the power to control the narrative about Black and Brown bodies in this country. Instead of silencing the voices of people of color, we need their help to guide us. I once had a friend admit to me that my opinions used to make him mad. He would get so frustrated with my repeated calls against racism and injustice in our country. But one day he realized that he had never tried to consider my point of view. He had been entirely focused on reacting to my words from his perspective as a white man. When he tried to see these same issues through my eyes, his entire stance shifted.

What if we asked the Black community what they think and feel the next time a Black man or woman is shot? What if, instead of jumping in to talk about grace, forgiveness, and reconciliation, we lament and listen to their rage and their pain?[8] What if, instead of redirecting the conversation to Black-on-Black crime or questioning whether race has anything to do with a killing, we open our hearts and listen to their stories, both what is said and what is unsaid? We cannot deconstruct racism in this country if we do not first go to the Black community and agree, "We must do something! So speak up!"

It's time for those in positions of power and privilege to internalize the voices and pleas of minorities and respond in the way they want you to respond. Relinquish control, listen to those on the margins, and choose to silence your own privileged opinion. Instead, hear what people directly impacted by the issue are saying.

Mourn the Way They Do

Put yourself in the shoes of a community where a young boy witnesses his father shot and killed by a police officer. What if it had been your dad? What if it was your spouse taken by ICE—and you never saw him or her again? What if your sister was forced against her will to undergo a hysterectomy in a detention center? What if you were falsely arrested and incarcerated?

I understand that issues like racism and systemic injustice are complex, and many Christians first turn to a political position for guidance on how to think or respond. But the issues we face are bigger than a political party. Regardless of who you support politically, we, as Christians, must learn how to walk in step with the Spirit, stepping into the shoes of the hurting person, taking on their humanity, and mourning for their pain.

Author Adrien Pei talks about how "the minority experience isn't primarily about head knowledge—but about emotional realities of *pain*."⁹ In other words, becoming a minority means embracing a filter of pain through which you view everything. It's not enough to simply discuss immigration policy or the killing of a person of color at an intellectual or theoretical level. You need to see that person's emotions and their pain around the problem. Immigration laws and your views on police aside, no matter who you are or what your circumstance is, there is always pain when a family is torn apart. Being judged because of your skin color causes pain. Being thought less of because you are poor causes pain. Being ostracized because you can't speak the dominant language very well causes pain. Being told that your only usefulness in

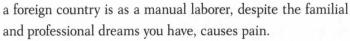

a foreign country is as a manual laborer, despite the familial and professional dreams you have, causes pain.

You need not only to recognize and acknowledge this pain but also to internalize it as your own. It's not easy to sympathize with people of other cultures. But our goal must be to grow in our ability to empathize, grieve, and lament with those who are hurting, no matter their ethnicity, nationality, or skin color.

Break Down Systems of Oppression as If They Were Your Own

Perhaps the hardest part of the conversation around justice for all is the question of how to challenge systems and the idea of reparations.[10] Many Christians have a difficult time believing that systemic, embedded causes of racism and injustice exist. It's hard to hear people tell you that you should take ownership for the sins of your forefathers. It's hard to hear people claim that current problems are not isolated to individuals but go deeper and reflect our country as a whole.

I hear many Christians say, "The past is the past," and "Things are getting better." Why should we have to keep rehashing things like the forced relocation of indigenous nations to reservations, the treatment of African people throughout our history (not only during the time of slavery but also in the present), the wrongful displacement of landowning Mexican Americans during Manifest Destiny at the hands of white Christians, and the forced relocation of Japanese Americans to concentration camps during World War II? The short answer? Because there are systems, attitudes, policies, structures, cultural patterns, and even laws in some cases that not only allowed these things to take place but continue to plague and traumatize people today. Most minorities in this country don't believe things have gotten better for them. The disparity between the dominant and subdominant cultures in our country is still shockingly large. If that is their perspective, it must be ours as well. If minorities believe that the systems in our country are continuing to hurt and oppress their communities, then we should listen and care about their interest in reforming and changing the systems we have.

If we want to change systems of injustice in our country, we need to have a broader, more communal understanding of our past. We need to see the history of Native Americans as our history. We need to see the history of African Americans, Asian Americans, and Latin Americans as our history too. Only when we gain their perspectives on the past will we be able to recognize that the wrongs committed in our nation's past still need to be accounted for. You will have a more fruitful time pursuing justice and engaging in conversations on unjust social structures and reparations if the experience of oppressed minorities in our country becomes deeply personal.

It's always easier to attend to our own issues. As an Asian American, I've had to call out the ways Asians have not always done a great job standing against anti-Black or anti–Native American racism. We have not been proximate to other communities of color and have often refused to stand in solidarity with them and their struggles. To a certain degree, we are all numb to other people's issues. But our numbness causes us not only to disengage in current cycles of racism and injustice but also to help perpetuate them.

So hear me: if you are white, challenge your mind and your heart to better hear and understand the lives and pain of people of color. If you are a person of color, learn how to step into the lives of those in other ethnic groups. Fellow friends of color, I know you've experienced pain, and it's hard to get your head above water when you feel like you're drowning. But we have to. We have to care about the systemic pains of other cultural groups. We have to step into their shoes and see how our experiences are far more interconnected than we realize. White people need to fight the systems of oppression against Black people. Asian Americans need to fight the systems of oppression against Native Americans. Latinos need to fight the systems of oppression against Asian Americans. We have to tackle every system of oppression as if it were our own.

The gospel has always been about this, about becoming all things to all people. The words of Scripture challenge us to step into other people's histories and stories, to see through their eyes, to mourn for their pain, and to build better futures for one another. Justice is not a distraction from the gospel. It is a core message of the gospel. The life of Jesus declares this to be true, and if you want to prioritize the gospel in your life, then the pursuit of justice on behalf of others must be an essential component of your faith. Like Paul, *become* the weak. See the world through their eyes. Only then will people truly begin to see Christ in you.

Conclusion

Don't Give Up

Some days I'm tired.

Choosing to adapt myself to others again and again is tiring. It's *especially* tiring when my efforts are not reciprocated. It would be easier if everyone was on the same page and if we were all excited to learn in humility and to respond to the needs of the people around us. But that doesn't happen as often as I would like.

But I'm still here, weary and trying to convince those stuck at step one, or those unwilling to begin this journey, that this is the only way forward. I'm still having conversation after conversation with people who don't see themselves as part of the problem when it comes to broken relationships across cultures, and it's exhausting. I'm also mocked and brushed aside on more occasions than I can count.

That's the hard reality.

Despite our best efforts, despite waking up each morning and choosing to do all we can to connect with the people around us, things won't always work out as planned. There will be pain, shame, and frustration. Real wounds. Some people in your life, no matter how much you adapt for them, are never going to adapt back. There will be people who call you crazy and probably a lot of other names that aren't appropriate to write down.

You also might end up stepping on toes and causing real pain. You might really mess things up, insulting instead of connecting. We can't always assume our best intentions will lead to effective outcomes.

Choosing a life where we seek to become all things to all people, as the apostle Paul challenges us to in 1 Corinthians 9:19–23, won't be easy. In fact, it might be the hardest thing you ever do. You'll feel discouraged on more than one occasion. You'll get hurt, angry, disheartened, perhaps even calloused along the way. You'll crash and burn and have scrapes and scars to show. So the question is not: Will this be hard? The question is: Are you willing to go the distance?

It's no accident that after Paul challenges us to be all things to all people, he draws an analogy to running a race. In 1 Corinthians 9:24–26 we read, "Do you not know that in a race all the runners run, but only one gets the prize? Run in such a way as to get the prize. Everyone who competes in the games goes into strict training. They do it to get a crown that will not last, but we do it to get a crown that will last forever. Therefore, I do not run like someone running aimlessly; I do not fight like a boxer beating the air." We're running a marathon, friends. There's no quick prize when it comes to cross-cultural relationships. You have to be in this for the long haul.

Athletes and runners sacrifice a lot to win a race. You and I need to be willing to forgo much in order to achieve healthy, flourishing relationships across cultural lines. The world of athletes speaks to the cost and the pain of what Paul is proposing. Prizes must be worked for, and the way is hard, humbling, and painful.

So we have to keep going.

Remember: it was never about us anyway. It's not about our rights, our privilege, our comforts, or our preferences. Cross-cultural relationships are all about the changes we need to make to connect across cultures. It's about continuing to mold and discipline our thoughts, our hearts, and our actions, in the words of Paul.

And this work won't happen overnight. You need to be patient with yourself and with everyone else. Even when Paul wrote 1 Corinthians 9:19–23, he hadn't reached the finish line. His journey was not yet over. You might feel like you've connected well with one person, only to realize you have a long way to go with someone else. You may be incredibly humble and flexible on one occasion and lose your cool the next time. You might have to move to a new state, start a new job, or switch churches, and the process will begin all over again. I know I'm not where I was ten years ago in my own understanding of cultural identities and how to relate with all peoples. I know I won't be the same ten years from now either. You won't be either.

More than that, we have to wholly believe that this pursuit isn't "aimless" (v. 26). This is not just an arbitrary lifestyle. Rather, it has everything to do with the gospel. Learning to culturally adapt ourselves is done in the pursuit of making Christ great and manifest in our lives. It's about fully living our calling as followers of Jesus.

Don't quit. None of this will be easy. But we can press on and be patient. We run the race for the promise of God's reward. And it will be worth the effort.

Acknowledgments

This book exists because people told me that my story mattered and that I should share it with the world. Friends, family, neighbors, colleagues—the people who were wrestling with how to connect across cultures and believed that I had something unique to offer within this conversation. I would like to first acknowledge and thank every person who encouraged me to speak into this space and to offer insights and experiences about cross-cultural relationships through my own Indian American lens.

I want to thank the Redbud Writers Guild for supporting my journey as a writer. I'm especially grateful for Ashley Hales and Bronwyn Lea, who both offered encouragement in the early days of book writing. I also want to thank my Redbud writers group—Janna Northrup, Stephanie Reeves, Sarah Hauser, Leah Everson, and Liz Charlotte Grant—for their feedback and assistance in each of my chapters. Thank you to Dorina Lazo Gilmore-Young and Tasha Jun Burgoyne, my fellow Asian American writers, for countless hours of discussion about writing styles, tone, and both the joys and struggles of discussing cultural identities as Asian American women.

I would like to thank Don Gates, my literary agent, for encouraging the book idea. Thank you for your support and guiding me through all the steps and details of the publishing world. And thank you, Zondervan, for your commitment to bringing more books on race and culture to Christian publishing.

I would like to thank Dr. Brian Howell and Dr. Alexander Jun, who both read select chapters of my manuscript and provided valuable insights into the different nuances and definitions of culture.

I am overwhelmingly grateful for each person who helped me process my book concept, title, and cover design. Many thanks to my friends Raymond Chang and Josh Buck for important phone calls and conversations, as well as Helen Lee, whose insights helped me craft the final title. Thank you, Jeff and Dana Johnson, as well as Mondo Scott, for offering invaluable creative insight to this project. I'm also grateful to JR Forasteros, whose encouragement and feedback along this journey have been invaluable. Thank you also to all my fellow (in)courage contributors and many more friends from Hope Community Church who were willing to give thoughts and feedback on both title and design, including Landon Wolford, Josh and Crystal Posada, Frank and Daniela Espinoza, and Rondell and Laura Trevino.

And, of course, my dear Chai Ladies—Sherrene DeLong, Sandhya Oaks, Ruby Varghese, and Leah Abraham—who cheered me on every step of the way and understood the heart of this book in a way that only fellow Indian American women can.

I want to thank my family because I would be a poor, starving author without their support. More than that, this book probably never would have been written without the countless hours that my parents, Andy and Anjana Linton, and my in-laws, Ron and Kathy Wilhite, watched our kids and all the times they sent over meals so I could write. Mom and Dad, I told you in kindergarten that I wanted to grow up and become a writer. Thank you for always supporting this dream.

I also want to thank all the incredible women in our church—Autumn Cleaves, Carla Hernandez, Victoria Trejo, Carolina Estrada, and Payton Crawley—who babysat our kids. Little did they know I would pick their brains and ask them countless questions about cultural identities and cross-cultural engagement. I'm indebted to their insight.

Finally, I want to thank my husband, Aaron, who has always believed in me, has always supported me, and has always been proud of me. You are my rock, now and always.

Notes

Introduction

1. J. Daniel Hays, *From Every People and Nation: A Biblical Theology of Race* (Downers Grove, IL: InterVarsity Press, 2003), 81.

2. Andrew Rillera, "Jesus' Multicultural Identity and Mission," November 17, 2020, https://www.madeforpax.org/storyarc. Rillera also notes, "Tamar was likely a Canaanite (Gen 38:2, 6), though later Jewish traditions hold she was an Aramean (north of Israel)."

Chapter 1: Develop Your Cultural Identity

1. Lecrae, interview by Ekemini Uwan, Christina Edmondson, and Michelle Higgins, *Truth's Table*, podcast, October 2017, https://soundcloud.com/truthstable/lecrae.

2. Academic texts that address cultural identity as ethnicity and story include Brian Howell and Jenell Paris, *Introducing*

Cultural Anthropology: A Christian Perspective (Grand
Rapids: Baker Academic, 2019); Sherry Ortner, *Anthropology
and Social Theory: Culture, Power, and the Acting Subject*
(Durham: Duke University Press, 2006); Michele de Certeu,
The Practice of Everyday Life (Berkeley: University of
California Press, 1988); Clifford Geertz, *The Interpretation
of Cultures* (New York: Basic Books, 1973); Marvin J. Newell,
*Crossing Cultures in Scripture: Biblical Principles for Mission
Practice* (Downers Grove, IL: InterVarsity Press, 2016);
Charles Taylor, *Modern Social Imaginaries* (Durham: Duke
University Press, 2003); and James K. A. Smith, *Desiring
the Kingdom: Worship, Worldview, and Cultural Formation*
(Grand Rapids: Baker Academic, 2009).

3. Georgia T. Chao and Henry Moon, "The Cultural Mosaic: A
Metatheory for Understanding the Complexity of Culture,"
Journal of Applied Psychology 90, no. 6 (2005): 1129.

4. For a more in-depth theological analysis of race throughout
Scripture, see J. Daniel Hays, *From Every People and Nation:
A Biblical Theology of Race* (Downers Grove, IL: IVP
Academic, 2003); as well as Kenneth A. Matthews and M.
Sydney Park, *The Post-Racial Church: A Biblical Framework
for Multiethnic Reconciliation* (Grand Rapids: Kregel
Academic, 2011).

5. To learn more about the intersection of ethnicity and faith,
see Sarah Shin, *Beyond Colorblind: Redeeming Our Ethnic
Journey* (Downers Grove, IL: InterVarsity Press, 2017), 25–41;
Orlando Crespo, *Being Latino in Christ: Finding Wholeness in
Your Ethnic Identity* (Downers Grove, IL: InterVarsity Press,
2009); Glenn Usry and Craig Keener, *Black Man's Religion:
Can Christianity Be Afrocentric?* (Downers Grove, IL: IVP
Academic, 2009); and Daniel Hill's concept of cultural
identity in *White Awake: An Honest Look at What It Means to
Be White* (Downers Grove, IL; InterVarsity Press, 2017).

6. Bruce Waltke, *Genesis: A Commentary* (Grand Rapids: Zondervan, 2001), 162.

7. See Richard Bauckham, *The Theology of the Book of Revelation* (Cambridge: Cambridge University Press, 1993), 33; and Hays, *From Every People and Nation*, 199.

8. See Craig Keener, *Revelation*, NIV Application Commentary (Grand Rapids: Zondervan, 2000), 195.

9. Sarah Shin, *Beyond Colorblindness: Redeeming Our Ethnic Journey* (Downers Grove, IL: InterVarsity Press, 2017), 6.

10. Malcolm X, "Message to the Grassroots," delivered on November 10, 1963, Detroit, MI.

11. Dorena Williamson, *ColorFull: Celebrating the Colors God Gave Us* (Nashville: B&H Kids, 2018).

12. The field of epigenetics has shown that historical and transgenerational trauma may be passed down through generations.

13. On resilience, see Sheila Wise Rowe, *Healing Racial Trauma: The Road to Resilience* (Downers Grove, IL: InterVarsity Press, 2020), 141–56.

14. Sam George, interview by Raymond Chang and Michelle Ami Reyes, *AACC Reclaim Podcast*, November 18, 2020, https://aaccreclaimpodcast.libsyn.com/.

Chapter 2: Move beyond Stereotypes

1. Social psychologists Shelley Taylor and Susan Fiske coined the term *cognitive miser* to describe our natural tendency to conserve cognitive resources. S. Taylor and S. Fiske, *Social Cognition* (New York: Random House, 1984). For more on how stereotypes are formed, see Craig McGarty, Vincent Y. Yzerbyt, and Russell Spears, "Social, Cultural and Cognitive Factors in Stereotype Formation," in *Stereotypes as Explanations: The Formation of Meaningful Beliefs about Social Groups* (Cambridge: Cambridge University Press,

2002); W. B. Mendes, J. Blascovich, S. Hunter, B. Lickel, and J. Jost, "Threatened by the Unexpected: Physiological Responses during Social Interactions with Expectancy-Violating Partners," *Journal of Personality and Social Psychology* 92 (2007): 698–716; and Christena Cleveland, *Disunity in Christ: Uncovering the Hidden Forces That Keep Us Apart* (Downers Grove, IL: InterVarsity Press, 2003), 44–45.

2. Nancy Wang Yuen, interview by Vivian Mabuni, *Someday Is Here*, podcast, November 10, 2020, http://www.vivianmabuni .com/someday-is-here.

3. On conciliation, see Mark Charles and Soong-Chan Rah, *Unsettling Truths: The Ongoing, Dehumanizing Legacy of the Doctrine of Discovery* (Downers Grove, IL: InterVarsity Press, 2019), 197–206; D. A. Horton, *Intensional: Kingdom Ethnicity in a Divided World* (Colorado Springs: NavPress, 2019), 17–34.

4. On the ethnic makeup of the New Testament world, see J. Daniel Hays, *From Every People and Nation: A Biblical Theology of Race* (Downers Grove, IL: IVP Academic, 2003), 141.

5. See, for example, Acts 28:4; Romans 1:14; 1 Corinthians 14:11; and Colossians 3:11.

6. F. F. Bruce, *Paul: Apostle of the Heart Set Free* (Grand Rapids: Eerdmans, 2000), 47.

7. Bruce, *Paul*, 47.

8. Hays, *From Every People and Nation*, 156.

9. Hays, *From Every People and Nation*, 142.

10. For more on the historical context of Corinth, see Paul Gardner, *1 Corinthians*, Exegetical Commentary on the New Testament (Grand Rapids: Zondervan, 2018), 17–36; Maria A. Pascuzzi, *First and Second Corinthians*, New Collegeville

Bible Commentary (Collegeville, MN: Liturgical, 2005), 5–15.

11. I use the term *cultural mosaic* from Georgia T. Chao and Henry Moon, "The Cultural Mosaic: A Metatheory for Understanding the Complexity of Culture," *Journal of Applied Psychology* 90, no. 6 (2005): 1128–40.

12. See Rakesh Kochhar and Anthony Cilluffo, "Key Findings on the Rise in Income Inequality within America's Racial and Ethnic Groups," *Pew Research Center*, July 12, 2018, https://www.pewresearch.org/fact-tank/2018/07/12/key-findings-on-the-rise-in-income-inequality-within-americas-racial-and-ethnic-groups/.

13. The myth of the model minority was created by white supremacists to pit Asian Americans against African Americans during the civil rights movement. To learn more about the history and purpose of this myth, read Ellen D. Wu's *The Color of Success: Asian Americans and the Origins of the Model Minority* (Princeton, NJ: Princeton University Press, 2014); also Moses Lee, "Asian Americans, MLK, and the Model Minority Myth," *The Witness* 7, September 2016, https://thewitnessbcc.com/asian-american-mlk-mode-minority/.

14. See Jacob Goldenberg et al., "We Look Like Our Names: The Manifestation of Name Stereotypes in Facial Appearance," *Journal of Personality and Social Psychology* 112, no. 4 (2017): 527–54.

15. Yara Simon, "Latino, Hispanic, Latinx, Chicano: The History behind the Terms," History, September 14, 2020, https://www.history.com/news/hispanic-latino-latinx-chicano-background.

16. To learn more, read Jon Aragon, "Double Punishment: Immigration and Anti-Blackness," World Outspoken, October

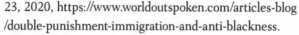

23, 2020, https://www.worldoutspoken.com/articles-blog
/double-punishment-immigration-and-anti-blackness.

17. MelindaJoy Mingo, *The Colors of Culture: The Beauty of
Diverse Friendships* (Downers Grove, IL: InterVarsity Press,
2020), 5.

Chapter 3: Embrace Cultural Discomfort

1. We almost always treat white culture as normal and evaluate
everyone else's culture based on the norms we associate
with white culture. As British sociologist Alistair Bonnet
says, "White culture is an unchanging and unproblematic
location, a position from which all other identities come
to be marked by their difference" ("White Studies: The
Problems and Projects of a New Research Agenda," *Theory,
Culture and Society* 13, no. 2 [1996]: 146). For more on white
default culture, see Beverly Daniel Tatum, *Why Are All
the Black Kids Sitting Together in the Cafeteria? And Other
Conversations about Race* (New York: Basic Books, 1997). On
white insulation from racial discomfort, see Robin DiAngelo,
*White Fragility: Why It's So Hard for White People to Talk
about Racism* (Boston, MA: Beacon, 2018).

2. I first learned of the term *cultural accommodation* from Paul
Gardner's exegetical commentary on 1 Corinthians and
find it incredibly useful for this discussion. See Gardner, *1
Corinthians*, Exegetical Commentary on the New Testament
(Grand Rapids: Zondervan, 2018), 403–17.

3. On the distinction between cultural relativism and moral
relativism, see Brian Howell and Jenell Paris, *Introducing
Cultural Anthropology: A Christian Perspective* (Grand Rapids:
Baker Academic, 2019), 48–52.

4. Adopting an outsider mentality as we practice cultural
accommodation is important because "each of the groups
cited in vv. 19–23 is an 'outsider' from the point of view of the

opposite group." Anthony C. Thiselton, *First Corinthians: A Shorter Exegetical and Pastoral Commentary* (Grand Rapids: Eerdmans, 2006), 144.

5. For more on white control over Black and Brown bodies, see Willie James Jennings, *The Christian Imagination: Theology and the Origins of Race* (New Haven, CT: Yale University Press, 2010); George Yancy, *Black Bodies, White Gazes: The Continuing Significance of Race in America* (Lanham, MD: Rowman & Littlefield, 2017); and Jemary Tisby, "Ahmaud Arbery Died for the Indefensible Principle of White Control," *Religion News Service*, May 8, 2020, https://religionnews .com/2020/05/08/ahmaud-arbery-died-for-the-indefensible -principle-of-white-control/.

Chapter 4: Rethink Code Switching, Privileges, and Rights

1. The term *enclothed cognition* was first used by Adam D. Galinksy in a 2012 *New York Times* article titled "Mind Games: Sometimes a White Coat Isn't Just a White Coat." See also Helene Pavlov, "Do the Clothes Make the Man (or Woman)?," *Huffington Post*, May 9, 2012, https://www .huffpost.com/entry/enclothed-cognition_b_1450687.

2. Carol Myers Scotton and William Ury first defined code switching in the 1970s as "the use of two or more linguistic varieties in the same conversation or interaction" ("Bilingual Strategies: The Social Functions of Code-Switching," *International Journey of the Sociology of Language* 13 [1997]: 7). The term has since been expanded upon to include nonverbal cues, such as body language and facial expressions. Deric Greene and Felicia Walker, for example, argued that code switching involves alternation between different communicative conventions ("Recommendations to Public Speaking Instructors for the Negotiation of Code-Switching

Practices among Black English-Speaking African American Students," *Journal of Negro Education* 73, no. 435 [October 2004]). More recently, Chao and Moon have utilized the theory of the cultural mosaic to argue that the term *code switching* should be replaced with the more comprehensive term *frame switching* in order to show how people adapt their entire identity, including how they act and talk. See Georgia T. Chao and Henry Moon, "The Cultural Mosaic: A Metatheory for Understanding the Complexity of Culture," *Journal of Applied Psychology* 90, no. 6 (2005) 1132.

3. See Mary Louise Pratt and her discussion of transculturation in *Imperial Eyes: Travel Writing and Transculturation* (New York: Routledge, 1992).

4. Paul Gardner, *1 Corinthians*, Exegetical Commentary on the New Testament (Grand Rapids: Zondervan, 2018), 403.

5. For more on this, see Dale B. Martin, *The Corinthian Body* (New Haven, CT: Yale University Press, 1995).

6. As Anthony C. Thiselton argues, "Paul explains that this comes not merely from a series of spontaneous, warmhearted gestures, but from a *settled strategy* that involves personal cost, '*doing without*' and keeping one's eyes on the goal" (*First Corinthians: A Shorter Exegetical and Pastoral Commentary* [Grand Rapids: Eerdmans, 2006], 145).

7. Gardner, *1 Corinthians*, 403.

8. Kathy Khang, *Raise Your Voice: Why We Stay Silent and How to Speak Up* (Downers Grove, IL: InterVarsity Press, 2018).

9. *Double Consciousness* is a term coined by W. E. B. Du Bois in the Atlantic Monthly article "Strivings of the Negro People" (1897). He writes, "[It's] a peculiar sensation, this double-consciousness, this sense of always looking at one's self through the eyes of others, of measuring one's soul by the tape of a world that looks on in amused contempt and pity. One ever feels his two-ness, an American, a Negro; two souls,

two thoughts, two unreconciled strivings; two warring ideals in one dark body, whose dogged strength alone keeps it from being torn asunder" (2).

10. I've been particularly encouraged by Osheta Moore's *Dear White Peacemakers* ministry. Her book, *Shalom Sistas: Living Wholeheartedly in a Brokenhearted World* (Harrisonburg, VA: Herald, 2017), as well as her podcast, *Shalom Y'all*, also explore how to pursue peace in the midst of racial hostility.

11. Martin Luther King Jr. spoke these words in April 1967 at New York's Riverside Church.

12. Ijeoma Oluo, *So You Want to Talk about Race* (New York: Seal, 2018), 57.

13. Oluo, *So You Want to Talk about Race*, 65–66.

Chapter 5: Avoid Cultural Appropriation

1. Roxana Hadadi, "Alison Roman, the Colonization of Spices, and the Exhausting Prevalence of Ethnic Erasure in Popular Food Culture," *Pajiba*, May 9, 2020, https://www.pajiba.com /celebrities_are_better_than_you/alison-roman-and-the -exhausting-prevalence-of-ethnic-erasure-in-popular-food -culture.php.

2. Rap music is frequently used as a positive example of cultural appropriation. However, this example is complicated by past and present power dynamics. Rap music was born from the rhythmic storytelling tradition of West Africa. Brought to the West by slaves, these rhythmic words wove their way through blues, jazz, and call-and-response and eventually birthed rap. From West Africa through slavery, the horror of the post-Reconstruction era, Jim Crow segregation, and post-Reagan mass incarceration, music has provided solace, hope, release, and strength to Black people. Yet for all that Black music gave to Black Americans, it was long vilified by many in white America, until white artists began imitating it—and then

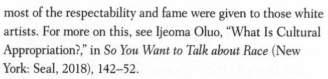

most of the respectability and fame were given to those white artists. For more on this, see Ijeoma Oluo, "What Is Cultural Appropriation?," in *So You Want to Talk about Race* (New York: Seal, 2018), 142–52.

3. Legal protection against cultural theft is still an important, if secondary, conversation to have. Cultural appropriation legal expert Susan Scafidi offers an illuminating and interdisciplinary conversation about the importance of cultural products in American life and their need for legal protection in *Who Owns Culture? Appropriation and Authenticity in American Law* (New Brunswick, NJ: Rutgers University Press, 2005).

4. For an extensive definition and discussion of cultural appropriation, see Bruce Ziff and Pratima V. Rao, eds., *Borrowed Power: Essays on Cultural Appropriation* (New Brunswick, NJ: Rutgers University Press, 1997).

5. Andray Domise, "How to Talk about Cultural Appropriation," *Maclean's*, September 21, 2016, https://www.macleans.ca /society/how-to-talk-about-cultural-appropriation/.

6. Navneet Alang, "Must We Forfeit Our Ghee?," *Hazlitt*, April 2, 2015, https://hazlitt.net/blog/must-we-forfeit-our-ghee.

7. Paul Gardner, *1 Corinthians*, Exegetical Commentary on the New Testament (Grand Rapids: Zondervan, 2018), 277.

8. On self-restraint in 1 Corinthians 9:19–23, see Anthony C. Thiselton, *First Corinthians: A Shorter Exegetical and Pastoral Commentary* (Grand Rapids: Eerdmans, 2006),47.

9. Gardner, *1 Corinthians*, 277–78.

10. Ta-Nehisi Coates has argued that gentrification is but a more pleasing name for white supremacy. See, for example, Coates, *We Were Eight Years in Power* (New York: One World, 2018), 86; also Coates, "A Hard Look at Gentrification," *The Atlantic*, July 21, 2011, https://www.theatlantic.com/national /archive/2011/07/a-hard-look-at-gentrification/242286/. Ibram

X. Kendi has also spoken out on the harm of gentrification in an interview with the *Washingtonian* (Rob Brunner, "Interview: Ibram X. Kendi Takes a Hard Look at Racism—and Himself," *Washingtonian*, October 23, 2019, https://www.washingtonian.com/2019/10/23/iibram-kendi-how-to-be-an-antiracist/).

11. Michelle Warren, *The Power of Proximity* (Downers Grove, IL: InterVarsity Press, 2017), 42.

Chapter 6: Don't Expect People to Come to You

1. Alan Henry and Rebecca Fishbein, "The Science of Breaking Out of Your Comfort Zone (and Why You Should)," *LifeHacker*, September 26, 2019, https://lifehacker.com/the-science-of-breaking-out-of-your-comfort-zone-and-w-656426705.

2. In the NIV Application Commentary on *1 Corinthians* (Grand Rapids: Zondervan, 1995), Craig Blomberg argues, "For many Western Christians living and working in relatively homogeneous secular settings, the most important lesson from verses 19–27 may relate to their choices of companions, whom they spend significant time with, cultivating friendships, and engaging in recreation or leisure-time pursuits" (188).

3. Alina Tugend, "Tiptoeing Out of One's Comfort Zone (and of Course, Back In)," *New York Times*, February 11, 2011, https://www.nytimes.com/2011/02/12/your-money/12shortcuts.html?pagewanted=all&_r=0.

4. For more on contact theory and the ways in which cross-cultural context is an exercise in error reduction, see Christena Cleveland, "Creating Positive Crosscultural Interactions," *Disunity in Christ: Uncovering the Hidden Forces That Keep Us Apart* (Downers Grove, IL: InterVarsity Press, 2003), 152–76.

5. For more on this, see Sherwood G. Lingenfelter and Marvin K. Mayers, Ministering Cross-Culturally (Grand Rapids:

Baker Academic, 2016), 15; Köstenberger and O'Brien, *Salvation to the Ends of the Earth: A Biblical Theology of Mission*, New Studies in Biblical Theology (Downers Grove, IL: InterVarsity Press, 2001), 181.

6. Willie James Jennings, *The Christian Imagination: Theology and the Origins of Race* (New Haven, CT: Yale University Press, 2011), 58.

7. Walter Brueggemann, *The Land: Place as Gift, Promise and Challenge in Biblical Faith* (London: SPCK, 1977), 5.

8. See Ashley Hales, "Oh, the Places We Will Stay," *Christianity Today*, June 14, 2019, https://www.christianitytoday.com /ct/2019/may-web-only/oh-places-well-stay-theology-of-place .html.

9. Martin J. Newell, *Crossing Cultures in Scripture: Biblical Principles for Mission Practice* (Downers Grove, IL: InterVarsity Press, 2016), 249.

10. Culture shock is defined by Paul Hiebert as "the sense of confusion and disorientation we face as we move into another culture" (*Anthropological Insights for Missionaries* [Grand Rapids: Baker Academic, 1986], 37). He also writes about "the disorientation we experience when all the cultural maps and guidelines we learned as children no longer work" (66).

11. Louise O. Fresco, "Why We Eat Together: Communal Dining Is a Quintessential Human Experience," *The Atlantic*, November 26,. 2015, https://www.theatlantic.com /entertainment/archive/2015/11/dinners-ready/416991/.

Chapter 7: Redefine Fluency

1. This is, essentially, the homophily principle. To learn more, read Miller McPherson, Lynn Smith-Lovin, and James M. Cook, "Birds of a Feather: Homophily in Social Networks," *Annual Review of Sociology* (August 2001) 27: 415–44.

2. Randy Woodley, *Living in Color: Embracing God's Passion for Ethnic Diversity* (Downers Grove, IL: IVP, 2001), 18–19.

3. David W. Pao, *Colossians and Philemon*, Exegetical Commentary on the New Testament (Grand Rapids: Zondervan, 2012), 228.

4. The word *barbarian* here is simply a transliteration in English from the Greek term. However, the basic meaning of the word *barbarian* doesn't hold the same connotations as it does today. We are not to assume that Paul intended to label this cultural group as less civilized. For more on this distinction, see Ben Witherington III, *The Acts of the Apostles: A Socio-Rhetorical Commentary* (Grand Rapids: Eerdmans, 1998), 776.

5. See Christena Cleveland, *Disunity in Christ: Uncovering the Hidden Forces That Keep Us Apart* (Downers Grove, IL: InterVarsity, 2003), 126–35.

6. This is what Craig Blomberg refers to as "friendship evangelism" in *1 Corinthians*, NIV Application Commentary (Grand Rapids: Zondervan, 1995), 188.

7. Witherington, *Acts of the Apostles*, 777.

8. Howell and Paris, *Introducing Cultural Anthropology*, 72.

9. Cleveland, *Disunity in Christ*, 127.

10. Arie Kruglanski has studied a phenomenon called cognitive closure, which is defined as an individual's "need for a firm answer to a question, any firm answer as opposed to confusion and/or ambiguity." Kruglanski, *The Psychology of Closed Mindedness* (New York: Psychology Press, 2004), 6.

11. See Matthew Lynch, "Talented and Gifted Learning: Where's the Diversity?," *Education Week*, September 4, 2013, http://blogs.edweek.org/edweek/education_futures/2013/09/talented_and_gifted_learning_wheres_the_diversity.html.

12. Ray L. Birdwhistell first coined the term *kinesics*, which he defined as "the study of body-motion as related to the non-verbal aspects of interpersonal communication" (*Kinesics*

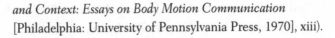

and Context: Essays on Body Motion Communication
[Philadelphia: University of Pennsylvania Press, 1970], xiii).

Chapter 8: Change Your Perspective on Justice

1. The concept of narrative justice has been used and developed
   in global health initiatives that aim to allow indigenous
   people to claim and tell their own stories. In *I See You: How
   Love Opens Our Eyes to Invisible People* (Downers Grove, IL:
   InterVarsity Press, 2019), Terence Lester defines narrative
   justice as the practice of taking the mic from the dominant
   voice and handing it over to the voices on the margins.
   Examples of this concept in action include filmmaker Lisa
   Russell's 2017 TED Talk titled "Promoting Responsible
   Storytelling in Global Health," Australia's Dulwich Centre's
   "narrative therapy," the "Charter of Storytelling Rights," and
   discussions on "story equity" by activist Judithe Registre, who
   is currently working on global poverty reduction.
2. Ken Wytsma, *The Myth of Equality: Uncovering the Roots of
   Injustice and Privilege* (Downers Grove, IL: InterVarsity Press,
   2017), 157.
3. I also recognize that the term *racism* is complex, and we need
   to have a proper working definition if we're going to confront
   and dismantle it together. To gain a clear definition of racism,
   I suggest you first read Ibram X. Kendi's *How to Be an
   Antiracist* (New York: One World, 2019); and Ijeoma Oluo's
   So You Want to Talk about Race (New York: Seal, 2018).
4. A useful overview and critique of Oppression Olympics is
   Andrea Smith, "Heteropatriarchy and the Three Pillars of
   White Supremacy: Rethinking Women of Color Organizing,"
   in *Feminist Theory Reader: Local and Global Perspectives*,
   ed. Carole R. McCann and Seung-kyung Kim (New York:
   Routledge, 2017), 273–81.

5. Paul Gardner, *1 Corinthians*, Exegetical Commentary on the New Testament (Grand Rapids: Zondervan, 2018), 408.

6. Gardner, *1 Corinthians*, 408.

7. Anthony C. Thiselton, *First Corinthians: A Shorter Exegetical and Pastoral Commentary* (Grand Rapids: Eerdmans, 2006), 147.

8. On the problem of quick forgiveness, see Dorena Williamson, "Botham Jean's Brother's Offer of Forgiveness Went Viral. His Mother's Call for Justice Should Too," *Christianity Today*, October 4, 2019, https://www.christianitytoday.com/ct/2019 /october-web-only/botham-jean-forgiveness-amber-guyger.html.

9. Adrian Pei, *The Minority Experience: Navigating Emotional and Organizational Realities* (Downers Grove, IL: InterVarsity Press, 2018), 7.

10. For a more extensive conversation on reparations, see Ta-Nehisi Coates, "The Case for Reparations," in *We Were Eight Years in Power* (New York: One World, 2018), 163–210. See also Duke Kwon's discussion on church reparation in his interview with Ekemini Uwan, Christina Edmondson, and Michelle Higgins, *Truth's Table*, podcast, March 2018, https:// soundcloud.com/truthstable/reparations-now-ecclesiastical -reparations-with-rev-duke-kwon; as well as "Q&A: Race Reparations with Pastor Duke Kwon," *Q Ideas* (2018), https:// qideas.org/race-reparations/.

Lightning Source UK Ltd.
Milton Keynes UK
UKHW041919010721
386493UK00001B/75